America's Tribute to Search and Rescue Dogs

T.F.H. Publications
One TFH Plaza
Third and Union Avenues
Neptune City, NJ 07753

ISBN 0-7938-0532-5

Distributed by T.F.H. Publications, Inc.

The American Kennel Club wishes to thank the following photographers for their work for this book:

Paul Bereswill, © The American Kennel Club – pages 13, 14, 16, 17, 20, 21, 22, 23, 24, 25, 26, 27, 30, 31, 32, 33, 34, 35, 36, 37, 41, 42, 43, 45, 48, 49 (inset), 50, 51, 52, 53, 54, 55, 56, 57, 58, 59, 62, 63, 64, 65, 66, 67, 70, 71, 72, 73, 74, 75, 76, 77, 78, 79, 82, 83, 84, 85, 86, 87, 88, 89, 90, 91, 92, 93, 94, 98, 100, 101, 102, 104, 105, 106, 107, 108, 110, 111, 114, 117, 118, 119, 120, 121, 122, 123, 125,

M Spano/Exact Photo © The American Kennel Club – pages 8, 9, 15, 18, 22, 28, 33 (inset), 35 (inset), 36 (inset), 38, 40, 44, 46, 49, 53 (inset), 60, 68, 80, 89 (inset), 95, 96, 99, 103, 112, 109, 115, 116, 124, 126, 128, 129

Emile Wamsteker for Rubenstein Associates Inc., © The American Kennel Club – pages 8, 9, 10, 11

New York Yankees – page 11

Book design by Candida Moreira Tomassini

www.tfh.com • www.akc.org • www.dogny.org

Table of Contents

STATE OF NEW YORK

GEORGE E. PATAKI
GOVERNOR

As Honorary Co-Chair of DOGNY, it is my privilege to introduce this wonderful tribute to the search and rescue dogs that came from all over the country to help New York in our hour of need. DOGNY is more than a tribute to these canine teams. It is our opportunity to give something back to the canine organizations, many of them volunteers, to help them train and prepare for the vitally important work they do for America.

I want to thank all the uniformed officers and the volunteers who brought their canine partners to New York. I also want to thank the American Kennel Club for organizing the DOGNY tribute, the artists who so brilliantly and lovingly decorated the dog sculptures, the sponsors who so generously supported this project and--most important--our canine friends who serve with such devotion.

Sincerely,

George Pataki

EXECUTIVE MANSION 138 EAGLE STREET ALBANY 12202

Preface

The American Kennel Club (AKC) is proud to present this volume of photographs and memories of *DOGNY – America's Tribute to Search and Rescue Dogs.*

For centuries, dogs have proved to be invaluable in rescuing humans lost or injured as a result of natural and man-made disasters. Nowhere was this more evident than after the Oklahoma City bombing in April 1995, and in the aftermath of the September 11, 2001 terrorist attacks. The DOGNY program was born from a desire to express appreciation for and pay tribute to search and rescue dogs and their handlers whose work is vital to our nation.

Flanked by an enthusiastic group of Midtown Manhattan firefighters on September 18, 2002, FDNY Commissioner Nicholas Scoppetta presented to the press a DOGNY sculpture fashioned into a toy fire truck. The setting for the event on the plaza in front of FAO Schwarz was a fitting venue for such an imaginative fusion of playfulness and respect.

Following the tragic events of September 11, 2001, The American Kennel Club pledged to assist the many canine search and rescue organizations that rely heavily on volunteers and donations for their existence. Over 90 canine search and rescue organizations participated in the aftermath of 9/11, and these organizations received over one quarter of a million dollars from donations that AKC collected for this purpose.

This positive effort pointed out very clearly that a permanent fund was needed to assist canine search and rescue organizations with vitally needed resources to respond to disasters, catastrophes, or crises. There is great value in being able to respond quickly to the needs of canine search and rescue teams when they are called upon in response to a tragedy. Heroes that they are, these selfless dogs and handlers cannot do it all on their own. In response to these needs, the Boards of The American Kennel Club and AKC Companion Animal Recovery (CAR) jointly agreed to create and support a permanent search and rescue relief fund for this specific purpose.

The AKC CAR Canine Support and Relief Fund was established as a permanent charitable fund to provide resources to search and rescue organizations responding to natural or civil disasters, to the veterinary units supporting them, and to not-for-profit shelters providing care to domestic animals displaced or orphaned by these disasters.

In response to this AKC fund-raising initiative, Dennis B. Sprung, Vice President of the AKC, conceived DOGNY as a

DOGNY artist Kristin Doney (second from right) joins students from The New York Institute for Special Education at Engine 76 on Manhattan's Upper West Side. The sculpture, titled "Celebrate Our NYC Heroes," includes tributes to search and rescue dogs in many languages, including Braille.

public art exhibition and fundraiser. DOGNY created over 100 life-sized sculptures of a German Shepherd Dog painted by artists with a special design for each dog. The sculptures were displayed for approximately three months in the summer and fall of 2002 at fire stations, police precincts, parks, and office buildings throughout New York City.

The American Kennel Club, AKC Companion Animal Recovery, and The Iams Company pledged to underwrite the expenses of DOGNY so that all funds donated would go toward the benefit of canine search and rescue organizations throughout the United States.

Transforming DOGNY from a concept to a public art exhibition involved the following key steps. First, there was the matter of creating a catalogue of artwork from which sponsors could choose designs for their sculptures. An open call for artists was conducted, and top arts organizations, galleries, and art schools in New York City were contacted. Artists saw DOGNY as an opportunity for creative expression while participating in an important cause. The response was overwhelming, with over 300 designs submitted for consideration to the AKC.

Finding sponsors to support DOGNY was the next challenge. The strength of the human-canine bond was clearly evident as corporations and individuals eagerly signed up to show their appreciation for the heroic dog-and-handler teams who worked so hard for our country.

Once sponsors chose their specific sculpture designs, the generosity of FedEx made it possible for blank sculptures to be brought to artists' studios throughout the Metropolitan New York area and back to the Williams Specialized Services in Hicksville, Long Island. Thanks

So many events made DOGNY a celebrated program in New York City. A press conference on June 25, 2002 brought members of the media to City Hall to hear AKC Chairman Ronald H. Menaker and New York City Mayor Michael R. Bloomberg announce DOGNY and debut its first sculpture. DOGNY co-chairs Dennis Sprung and Karen LeFrak look on.

DOGNY sculpture "The Heart to Save Mankind," by Donna Parker, on exhibit at the East River Esplanade, facing downtown.

A salute to DOGNY on the Great White Way unfolded at Shubert Alley on August 21, 2002. Cast members of the Broadway hit "Mamma Mia!"—Karen Mason, Louise Pitre, and Judy Kaye—gathered before the media to debut two sculptures called "Broadway Loves DOGNY" and "Show Stoppers," with AKC Chairman Ronald H. Menaker (far left), AKC President Alfred L. Cheauré (far right), and artist Billy (crouched).

to the logistical expertise of the Williams team, the sculptures were then assembled for transport to their destinations throughout the five boroughs of New York City. Following the exhibition, a number of DOGNY sculptures made their way to Sotheby's for auction by Liz Smith and Benjamin Doller, with the proceeds going to the AKC CAR Canine Support and Relief Fund.

AKC wishes to acknowledge the tremendous support from the following key corporate sponsors who were instrumental in the success of this important work: AKC Companion Animal Recovery Corporation, The Hartz Mountain Corporation, The Iams Company, FedEx, and JPMorgan Chase. In addition, the response to DOGNY from the public has been tremendous and heartwarming, with hundreds of individual sponsors and donors joining this worthy cause. Mayor Michael Bloomberg supported this program and its partnership with the City of New York. Co-Chairs Karen LeFrak and Dennis Sprung lent unparalleled focus to the program, which was bolstered by the indispensable support of our Honorary Chairmen Mayor Michael Bloomberg, Governor George Pataki, former Mayor Rudolph Giuliani, NYPD Commissioner Raymond Kelly, and FDNY Commissioner Nicholas Scoppetta.

This program has raised over two million dollars, proving once again that the love of dogs is present in the hearts of human beings everywhere.

Supermodel Heidi Klum showed her support for DOGNY as she unveiled her very own creation called "Dog With Butterflies" on September 27, 2002.

The powerful bond between children and dogs was witnessed in two events for DOGNY, both among the over 20 sculptures generously sponsored by The Iams Company. On October 14, 2002, patients in the Child Life Program at St. Vincent's Hospital in New York City painted a DOGNY sculpture, depicting the hopefulness of children everywhere.

There are dates in history that are forever ingrained in our national consciousness. Some of these dates celebrate great triumphs, while others commemorate unspeakable tragedies. September 11, 2001, is certainly one of the latter. Out of this tragedy has come a new spirit of selflessness and giving. Like all Americans, dog lovers have not been immune to these emotions. In the days, weeks, and months following 9/11, we took the opportunity to do something, when being able to do anything to help was so important to all of us. Our need to help, our love of dogs, and our understanding of the depth of the human-canine bond were ultimately the foundation for the great success of *DOGNY – America's Tribute to Search and Rescue Dogs.*

To all of you who have participated in our quest to support Canine Search and Rescue going forward, we sincerely thank you.

Ronald H. Menaker,
Chairman, AKC

Alfred L. Cheauré,
President/CEO, AKC

August 24, 2002 was DOGNY Day at Yankee Stadium. Broadway star Linda Eder sang the National Anthem. 25,000 special edition DOGNY toys fashioned in Yankee pinstripes were generously donated by The Hartz Mountain Corporation to all of the young fans that day. Pictured are (left to right) AKC Vice President Dennis B. Sprung, Hartz Mountain President Robert Devine, and AKC President Alfred L. Cheauré.

THE NEW YORK TIMES, TUESDAY, SEPTEMBER 10, 2002 A9

The American Kennel Club (AKC) proudly acknowledges the kind and generous contributions to DOGNY℠

DOGNY℠ serves as a living memorial to the thousands of precious lives that were lost in the attacks on our country on September 11, 2001. It is made possible through the support of corporations, organizations and individuals who, collectively, have donated more than $2 million to date.

Contributions are made to the American Kennel Club Companion Animal Recovery Corporation Canine Support and Relief Fund. Far into the future, these monies will help provide canine search and rescue organizations with the resources needed for dealing with a wide variety of emergencies and disasters.

In a spirit of national unity, we express our heartfelt thanks to the following:

MAJOR SPONSORS:
The Iams Company
The Hartz Mountain Company
FedEx
JPMorgan Chase
The American Kennel Club
American Kennel Club Companion Animal Recovery

CORPORATE, CLUB AND INDIVIDUAL SPONSORS:
A&P
Dr. and Mrs. Sheldon Adler
Ahold USA
Animal Medical Center
Animal Planet
The Atlanta Kennel Club, Inc.
Bank One
Bayer
Bollinger, Inc.
Canine Chronicle
Chain O'Lakes Kennel Club (Illinois)
The Chubb Group of Insurance Companies
D.B.O.
Deramus Foundation
Dog News
German Shepherd Dog Club of America
Gibson Dunn and Crutcher LLP
Walter F. Goodman
Harrisburg Kennel Club
Hill's Pet Nutrition
Sandra and Howard Hoffen, Monica, Tux and Michael
Insignia/ESG
Interbrand Corporation
Gilbert S. Kahn
Amy Kiell and Harvey Schwartz: Pebbles' Run Samoyeds
King Features Syndicate
Landor Associates
Janet Lange
Sam and Marion Lawrence
Lefrak Organization
Lehman Brothers
Little Fort Kennel Club
Loews Hotels
Howard M. Lorber
Linda and Mickey Low
Major League Baseball
Mr. and Mrs. Ronald Menaker
Merial
Nestlé Purina Petcare Company
New York Mets
News Corporation/New York Post
Laura J. Niles Foundation
NJ Pets
Novartis
Nutro Products, Inc.
Pace University
Park Shore Kennel Club
Pedigree/Master Foods USA
Jeffrey Pepper and the Stella and Arthur Pepper Foundation, Inc.
The Petco Foundation
Petland Discounts
Pfizer Animal Health Group
Philip Ross Industries
Corey and Alicia Pinkston
Marilyn Polite
Polo Ralph Lauren
Anne Radice in honor of Prof. Iris Love
Mr. and Mrs. Roger Rechler
Reckson Associates
Remington Arms Company
Daryl and Steven Roth Foundation
Cecelia Ruggles and J.R.
Saatchi and Saatchi
Santa Clara Valley Kennel Club
Mr. and Mrs. Martin Sosnoff
Springfield Kennel Club
John Spurling
Telford Veterinary Hospital
Triple Crown Dog Academy
Lillian Vernon Foundation
Veterinary Pet Insurance

CORPORATE, CLUB AND INDIVIDUAL CONTRIBUTORS:
Svetlana Adler
The AKC Call Center Staff
The Alaskan Malamute Club of America
Dolores Alonso
George and Mary Ann Alston
American Airlines
Charles and Sharon Anderson
Maria Andriano
Howard and Barbara Atlee
Kathleen and Roland Augustine
Mr. and Mrs. Roger N. Ayres
Joseph and Greer Baffuto
Drs. Mary Burch and Jon Bailey
Noreen and Carl Baxter
Joanne Mary Beacon
Tiffany Beard
Pamela Bennerson
Catherine Bell
George Berger
Tanya Bielski
William D. Birch
Bobby Birdsong
David and Phyllis Blevins
Eileen Bolton
Anne Bolus
Debra Ann Bonneford
Jesse and Galye Bontecou
Janet and Sanford Borinsky
E.G. and C.J. Brennan
Bronx County Kennel Club
Cara Imogene Buchicchio
Ms. Linda Lee Burke
David Buttgereit
Denise LeFrak Calicchio
Valarie and Delroy Campbell
Delaine W. Cantrell
Michael Allway and Anne C. Caplan
Wendy N. Carduner
Sue Cerbone
Jessie Chanoine
Alfred and Patricia Cheauré
Cine Magnetics, Inc.
Peter A. Cohen
Kristin Colvin
Jacqueline Cook
Sharon Cook
Stephen Costallos
James and Agnes Crowley
Tim Cunningham
Dennis and Arline Cutler
Nicholas and Rosalee D'Altilio
William G. and Cathy H. Daugherty
Davis Polk and Wardwell
Carrie DeYoung
Janet Ford and James Dearinger
Kirby and Bonita Dennis
Bernard Depinto
Jenny Dickinson
Barbara M. Dille
Gina DiNardo Lash and Marc D. Lash
Dog Show Photography: Tom and Cathi DiGiacomo
Doll-McGuinness
Janet Doolittle
Linda Duncklee
The DuPont Corporation Automotive Paint Division
R. Dean Eagle
Kim Eberley
Mrs. Henry D. Epstein
James and Sue Etheridge
Garadine Fair
Malina and Edward Farshtey
Sharon Faucette
Victoria Field and The AKC Learning and Development Department
Leslie Finch
Finger Lakes Kennel Club, Inc.
Clark Fiscella
Lester Fisher
The Flaherty Family Foundation
Charlotte Ford
Fort Worth Kennel Club
Valerie Franklin
Keith and Shannon Frazier
David and Cherilyn Frei
Albert A. Fried, Jr.
Kenny and Rita Fulmer
Frieda Furman
Peter and Terri Gaeta
Jan Gaff
Patricia Gallatin in honor of Ch. Friendship Hill Dr. Watson and Ernesto Lara
Rita Gardner
Patricia A. Gellerman
Mr. and Mrs. Peter Georgescu
Alice Gilibert
Tom Glassford and Robin Stansell
Judy Gold
Harvey and Susan Goldberg
Goldsmith Family Charitable Foundation, Inc.
Jerome R. Goldstein
Yvette Gonzalez
Murray Goodman
Rebecca Gordon
Tilly Grassa
Susan L. Gray
Greater Collin Kennel Club
Barbara Green
Helen Chrysler Greene
The Alan C. Greenberg Foundation
Kathryn Greer
Guenther E. and Renate Greiner
Terri Grodner
Jan L. Gross in memory of Diane Gross
Joyce Harris
Darrell and Doreen Hayes
Gerry and Perren Hayes
Dave and Peggy Helming
Theresa S. Hensgen
Skip and Jervia Herendeen in memory of Maxwell Riddle
Ninette Herron
Jean Hetherington
Gus N. Hinojosa, R.A.
William and Janet Holbrook
Mara C. Holiday
Carol J. Hollands
Anthony A. Houston
Tonya and Teddy Howe
Howard G. Hubbard
Debra A. Iles
Interzoo Show
Jill Iscol
Kandie K. Isom
Desiree Jaeger
Lyle and Marjorie Johnson
Sale F. Johnson
Jupiter-Tequesta Dog Club
Jasmina Kalamperovic
Peter Kalikow
George S. Kaufman in honor of Karen LeFrak
Kathy Kaye
Elisa Kelly
The Kennel Club Charitable Trust
Paul and Linda Kline
Denise Kodner
Barbara Jane Kolk
Kraftsman Group, Inc.
Patricia Krause
The H. Frederick Krimendahl II Foundation
Mary-Lee Kviecikus
Labrador Retriever Club
S.C. LaBrecque
Joan and Joe Lacey in honor of Karen LeFrak
Ed Lamberski
Christina Lang Assael
Langley Kennel Club
Cristyne F. Lategano
The Lauder Foundation
Patricia W. Laurans
Richard T. Leeolou
Chi-Ky Li
Michael A. Liosis
John Langloth Loeb, Jr.
Long Island Kennel Club
Cynthia and Dan Lufkin
Kim Dung Luong
Ninah and Michael Lynne
Elizabeth Mahncke
Pamela Cooper-Manatos and Cary Manatos
Anne and Thomas Maness
Maran's Autobody, Woodside, NY
Greg Martin
Marzocco Dun-Rite Autobody Inc.
Nancy Matlock
Ian and Sonnet McKinnon
Juanita and Mary Beth McMullen in honor of Treson
Theresa Holt-McNulty
Kelly J. Meehan
Patricia Meehan
Robert and Meryl Meltzer
The Middle Peninsula Kennel Club
Mrs. Barbara Miller
Howard P. Milstein Foundation
Barbara Moore
Linda C. More
Chappy Morris
Mountain Range Farms, L.P.
Albert and Cynthia Musciano
Carol J. Murray
Nashville Kennel Club
Carmen R. Nassar
National Ethnic Coalition of Organizations (NECO)
New Brunswick Kennel Club
Greg and Donna Newsome
Daniel Nitschke
Brenda Nix and Donna Pintye in memory of Odie
Barbara Ohmann
Daisy L. Okas
Onate Trail Dog Fanciers Association
Marie E. O'Neill
Margaret O'Reilly in memory of Shannon
Stephanie and Jeffrey Ortel
Pamela and Edward Pantzer
Pamela Pantzer
Sandra Parente in honor of John A. Parente
Rajshree S. Patel
Susan Patricof
Toni Peebler
Penn Ridge Kennel Club, Inc.
Pepsi Cola Company
Willie Perry
Alira Phillips
Robin Pickett in honor of Karen LeFrak
Stephanie Pier
Eileen Pimlott
Michael Pinero
Quarto, Inc.
Pauline and Morgan Radler
Ron and Suzanne Readmond
Vicki and Peter Rees
Regency, A Loews Hotel
Republic Mills, Inc.
Karen Reuter
Wendy Richardson
Elaine Ridgen
David and Ellen Roberts
Gary S. Robinson
Maria Robinson
Chris Rogers
Marshall Rose
Mr. and Mrs. Jonathan P. Rosen
Susan Rudin
Candace Russell
Emilia A. Saint-Amand
Kathleen Scherle
Lowell M. Schulman
Mr. and Mrs. Stephen A. Schwartzman
Virginia and Raymond Scott
Patricia Scully
Security Packaging Company, Inc.
Ann Sergi
Irving Shafran
Thomas and Ashley Sharp
Susan B. Sherman
Nancy and Henry Silverman
Simkins Industries, Inc.
Neil R. Singer
Robert H. Slay
Don and Elaine Sloan
Polly and Robert Smith
Somerset Hills Kennel Club
Larry Sorenson
Paul and Daisy Soros Foundation
Specialty Pet Supplies, Inc.
William and Matilda Speck
Peggy Speed
Maria Spencer
Dennis and Susan Sprung
Matthew H. Stander
Allison Stern
Charlotte St. Martin
Jackson Steele
James T. and Andrea Stevens
Daphna Straus
Bonnie and Tom Strauss
Christine Strom
Michael J. Suave
Alice Suriani
Michael F. Swick
Angeles Tay
Tina Thomas
Tiffany & Co.
The Laurie Tisch Sussman Foundation
Barbara and Donald Tober
Jacqueline Tomkovich
D. Kay and Ralph G. Tripp
Donald Trump
Pauline Tucker in honor of Karen LeFrak
Cleolo Vacula
M. VandenBergh
Michelle Veasey
Dawndolyn Walden
Ellen M. Walsh
Isabel Walsh
Jack Waltz
Larry and Donna Warsoff
Helma N. Weeks
Hilde Weihermann
James Weingartner
Ina West
John and Charlotte White
Wendy D. Williams
Kim Winston
Ruth Winston
Susan Elaine Winter
Betty Winthers in loving memory of Michele Simpson
Jean S. and Hugh M. Witt III
Meredith Wollins
John W. Woods
Reva Wurtzburger
The Janet Stone Jones Foundation on behalf of Janet York
Robert and Cindy Young

DOGNY has received Corporate Sponsorships and Corporate Contributions from companies that wish to remain anonymous.

AMERICAN KENNEL CLUB · AKC · INCORPORATED

Please make your tax-deductible contribution payable to:
AKC/CAR Canine Support and Relief Fund
Mail to: AKC/DOGNY, 260 Madison Avenue, New York, NY 10016
www.dogny.org

CAR Companion Animal Recovery

Flags of the World

Ana Sofia Vigas

About the Artwork:

"I have used this sculpture to represent the national flags of the 42 countries in which people lost their lives in the September 11 disaster."

About the Artist:

Ana Sofia Vigas painted two DOGNY sculptures to recognize "the importance that dogs play in our everyday lives and experiences." She resides in Brooklyn, New York.

Sponsor: Iams Dog Foods/The Iams Company

New York Patriot

C. M. Gross

About the Artwork:

"This piece depicts a young man watching the workers, police, and firefighters walking to and from the site of Ground Zero. This took place on West Street the weekend following the attacks. It was the closest I could get to the site, and the first time I was able to get into the city. The young man's face and spirit read complete loyalty and respect to everyone who was dedicating themselves to this disaster."

About the Artist:

"I have always been a 'real' New Yorker. This is due to the fact that I was born and have spent most of my life in Brooklyn. A true native in every sense of the word, I attended the High School of Art and Design, School of Visual Arts, Hunter College, and Pratt Institute, where I teach illustration. I am a freelance illustrator and painter. I am in several corporate and museum collections, including The Museum of The City of New York. I am proud of the fact that I come from the most ethnically diverse city in the world."

Rescue Workers

C. M. Gross

About the Artwork:

"The inspiration for Rescue Workers came from a poster in front of Saint Paul's Church on Broadway. While people waited on line to view Ground Zero from its newly built platform, I came to view the people. There must have been thousands of flyers around the city of missing loved ones, but few of rescue workers. One group of rescue workers I am proud to pay homage to are the rescue dogs. I myself am a dog owner and know how loyal and dedicated they are."

About the Artist:

"I have always been a 'real' New Yorker. This is due to the fact that I was born and have spent most of my life in Brooklyn. A true native in every sense of the word, I attended the High School of Art and Design, School of Visual Arts, Hunter College, and Pratt Institute, where I teach illustration. I am a freelance illustrator and painter. I am in several corporate and museum collections, including The Museum of The City of New York. I am proud of the fact that I come from the most ethnically diverse city in the world."

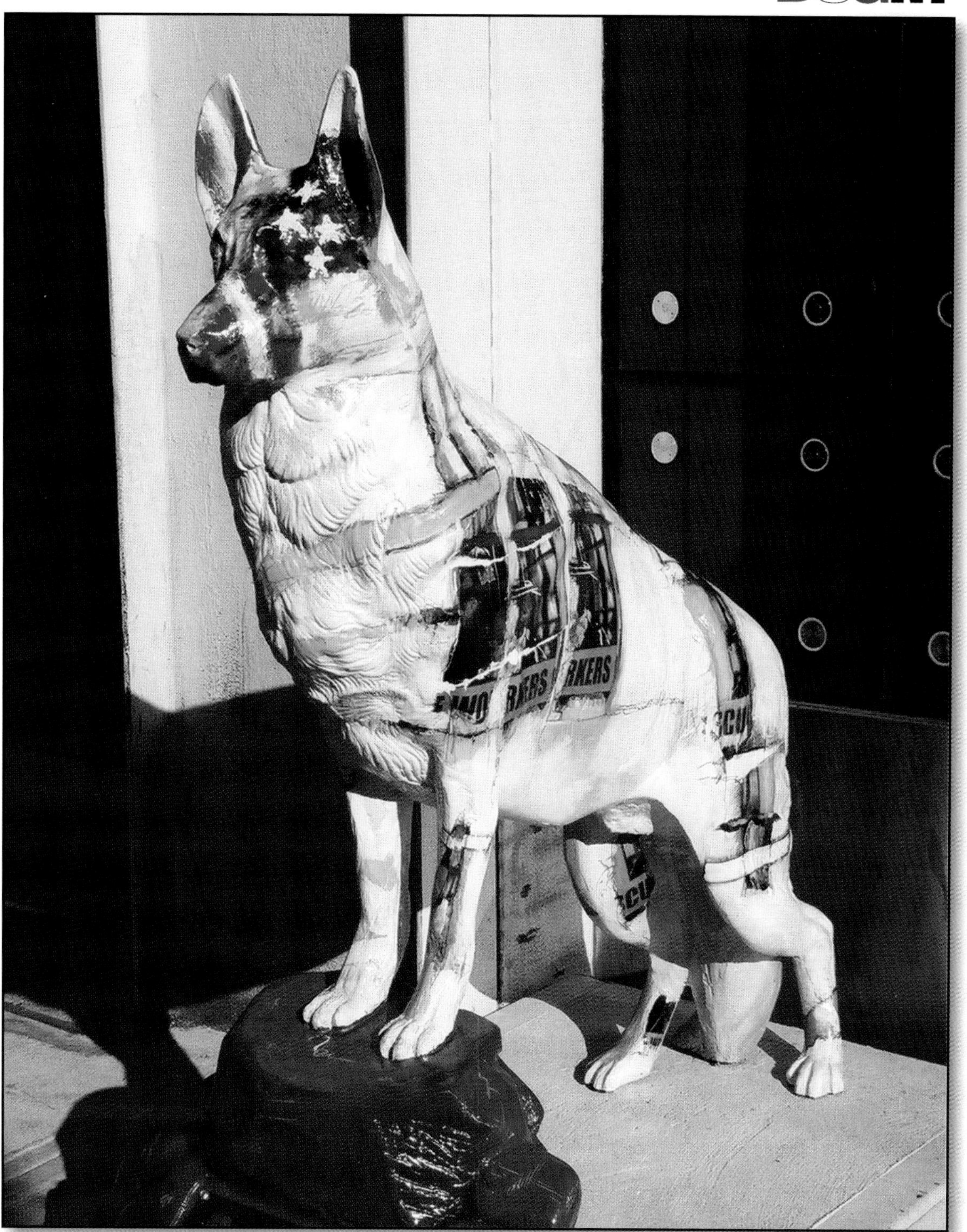

Sponsor: Dr. and Mrs. Sheldon Adler

Super Dog

Margaret Cherubin

About the Artwork:

"In his skin-tight suit, with his formidable muscles bulging, SuperDog is ready to take on all evildoers and bring good to the world. His cape and mask keep his true identity a secret On his cape is a dog head symbol—the symbol of bravery and goodness. Don't we all feel that the search and rescue dogs were all SuperDogs?"

About the Artist:

Margaret Cherubin announced at the age of two that she was an artist and has passionately maintained that identity throughout her life. Using dreams, myth, nature, and the rich associations they call up in her imagination, she works to touch the common threads that bind us together as human beings. Sculpting clay dug from the earth, participating in the fiery process that produces bronze, and carving into the natural colors and grains of aged wood or ancient stones, she uncovers what is already there, waiting to resonate within the observer.

Unsung Hero

Trystan Bates

About the Artwork:

"Unsung Hero is meant to serve as a token of respect and honor to rescue dogs, especially those employed during the recent months in New York. A secondary purpose of this piece is to remind people of the pride and love for our country that was displayed during the events of September 11th.

"It is my wish that this sculpture will reinforce the fact that one's pride and love for country should always be as strong as it was during those difficult days and, in addition, be extended throughout the globe, into all and by all nations, with the hope of working together as a united people toward a better future."

About the Artist:

After studying illustration at Parsons School of Design, Trystan Bates traveled to the Rietveld Acadamie in Amsterdam, Netherlands, where photography and fine art became his main focus. Upon returning to Manhattan, he became the chief coordinator at Felissimo Design House, as well as the US Associate Director for *ROJO* magazine, Barcelona. He continues to produce personal pieces rooted in fine art and photography for exhibition both in the US and abroad.

Major

Claudia Vosper

About the Artwork:

Major League Baseball's dog, Major, combines découpage and acrylic paint into a lively and eclectic comic-book-style storyboard that unites the excitement of the World Series with the noble lifesaving efforts of New York City's search and rescue dogs.

"We decided to use Major League Baseball's official superhuman artwork to reflect the incredible efforts of the search and rescue dogs in the weeks after 9/11," artist Claudia Vosper says. "And on a personal note, having seen the actual rescue dogs at work at Ground Zero, I felt fortunate to be able to participate in honoring these true heroes."

About the Artist:

California native Claudia Vosper graduated from California State University at Long Beach with a BFA in Visual Communication, then moved to New York City soon after to pursue a career in graphic design. After 12 years as an art director in advertising and various design studios, Claudia landed in Major League Baseball's Design Services department, where she was given the opportunity to head up the DOGNY contribution.

Manhattan Guide Dog

Gordon M. Sasaki

About the Artwork:

"This work is inspired by the unwavering faithfulness of search and rescue dogs to provide direction in times of crisis. This design reflects the tremendous support that these dogs gave to the people who suffered losses on 9/11. This model will act as a useful map for those lost in our city and provide valuable information and direction to the public in their time of need."

About the Artist:

"I am a professional artist with a special connection to the bond between humans and canines. Since having suffered a spinal cord injury from an automobile accident, resulting in paralysis and the need for a wheelchair for mobility, I have depended on the physical and spiritual support that service dogs provide. My experience with such animals and the unconditional love they give makes me excited to participate in this project, and I am especially sympathetic to the New York City police officer who lost his dog/partner in the World Trade Center disaster."

My Co-Pilot

Denise Shaw

About the Artwork:

"Inspired by the *Bark* magazine slogan, 'Dog is my Co-Pilot' (dog is God spelled backwards), our own beloved German Shepherd mix Nick is the model for this sculpture. Nick's emblem on the back of his jacket, 'Nick, Search and Rescue Ace,' is inspired by flamboyant artwork that often decorated the fronts and backs of A2 leather flight jackets in World War II. It frequently replicated the nose art painted on the wearer's aircraft. There's a patch on the front of Nick's jacket that says 'The Spirit of St. Nick.' The rubble on which he stands has been transformed into a piece of sky."

About the Artist:

Denise Shaw's work has been exhibited throughout the US, including A.I.R. Gallery, Paula Cooper Gallery, the Swiss Institute in New York City, Woodruff Arts Center in Atlanta, Georgia, and the University of North Carolina in Charlotte. Her work was included in *Time Capsule: A Concise Encyclopedia by Women Artists*, published by Creative Time. Ms. Shaw received a Bachelor of Fine Arts from the School of Visual Arts and a Certificate in Film at New York University.

Stars & Stripes

Carol A. Massa

About the Artwork:

"My design was inspired from the spirit and courage of 'Our Men & Dogs,' working together. Watching people and dogs never stopping in search of survivors gave me chills. My patriotism was touched deeply to feel our country as one. To see our flags hanging from every spot in the city gave me the feeling that led to this design."

About the Artist:

"I live and work in the heart of Greenwich Village. I have many stages of works, from classical etchings and drawings to abstract paintings. I have been painting since 1980. My style is abstract expressionism. In the act of painting, I am involved with movement and stillness, color and texture, all of which reflect my personal journey. Working with rhythmic marks from brush and roller, I am able to release energetic gestures. This method allows freedom and spontaneity in creating my images."

Many Nations, One Mission

Tom Cappelletti

About the Artwork:

"When disaster or tragedy strikes, no matter where, search and rescue dogs and their handlers are deployed from many nations to any nation that may be in need. It is such a universal humanitarian response to others in need, and symbolic of our higher natures and true caring for all mankind. The collage of flags represent the many nations of the world, recognizing nations that provide and those that receive the services of SAR dogs—mankind coming together using man's best friend for universal good."

About the Artist:

"I am a graphic artist and illustrator here in New York City. I'm a graduate of UCLA's School of Design. I am in business with my sister, Sandy, also an artist. We've provided original art for wall décor and greeting card manufacturers since 1996. Our designs have appeared as greeting cards, note cards, and framed art at a variety of retailers, as well as products from fine stationery to boxer shorts. I have also worked as an art director and visual stylist on numerous motion pictures, music videos, commercials, and photo shoots."

Once Upon a Time

Ana Sofia Vigas

About the Artwork:

"The reason I chose to draw the city skyline of New York City on the sculpture of this dog is that the strong lines of the buildings align with the proud, alert stance of the dog, which shows the beauty and strength of this amazing animal in contrast to the hard lines. I have chosen the warm pastel colors that are familiar in New York City and which people associate with dogs. This makes the picture friendly and approachable and makes it stand out."

About the Artist:

Ana Sofia Vigas painted two DOGNY sculptures to recognize "the importance that dogs play in our everyday lives and experiences." She resides in Brooklyn, New York.

Our Thanks

Susan Jacob

About the Artwork:

"This design was inspired by the numerous photographs after September 11th of people in profile. You need not see their face to know their feelings of that day—gestures say enough. This woman, in a Rorschach-like design, is giving thanks to the people who worked so hard on site, supported from afar, and were victims of this event. It also expresses our thanks that this great country has not fallen apart and that we are able to carry on."

About the Artist:

"My background in art began at a very young age. I always had access to paint, and about the same time I started to show dogs, my art became serious. So, throughout high school I filled my curriculum with art courses and entered many competitions. I received a Gold Key Scholastic Art Award in painting in 2000, a Silver Key in Sculpture in 1996, and Honorable Mentions in painting in 1998 and 1999. I also have published artwork in the *AKC Gazette* in the September 2001 issue and the 2001-2002 Christmas subscription campaign. I continue to explore my range as a visual artist even while attending North Carolina School of the Arts School of Filmmaking."

Unending Tear

Cecelia Holmes

About the Artwork:

"What struck me as I viewed the news of the World Trade Center was the way the rescue workers went through the days and nights following the collapse, searching for survivors. At their side stood the search and rescue dogs. The bond between handler and dog was and still is a wonderful thing to behold. These rescue dogs gave so much. I cried when I read how despondent they became when they found no survivors, but I reveled in the fact that their presence helped the rescue workers survive the tragedy to which they bore witness. My friend W. S. DeWitt was involved with the painting of the piece. Our hearts were within each stroke of the brush, for our tears over this tragedy of the World Trade Center are unending, and we want the world to see that magical bond that we bore witness to between the search and rescue dogs, their handlers, and all workers at the site."

About the Artist:

"I am a watercolorist, reviewed by *Newsday* when I was in school as an up-and-coming artist."

St. Vincent's Loves DOGNY

Children of the Child Life Program

About the Artwork:

Painting the DOGNY sculpture was an enormous benefit to the children at St. Vincent's Hospital. It gave them a sense of pride to be able to take part in this citywide art project and also provided them with a distraction from their illnesses.

About the Artists at St. Vincent's Hospital:

The Child Life Program at St. Vincent's Hospital in Manhattan provides psychological, social, and emotional support for hospitalized children. The program strives to ease the stress of hospitalization through play, art, and other therapeutic activities. The kids who participated in the project were in-patients, outpatient children with chronic illnesses, and their siblings.

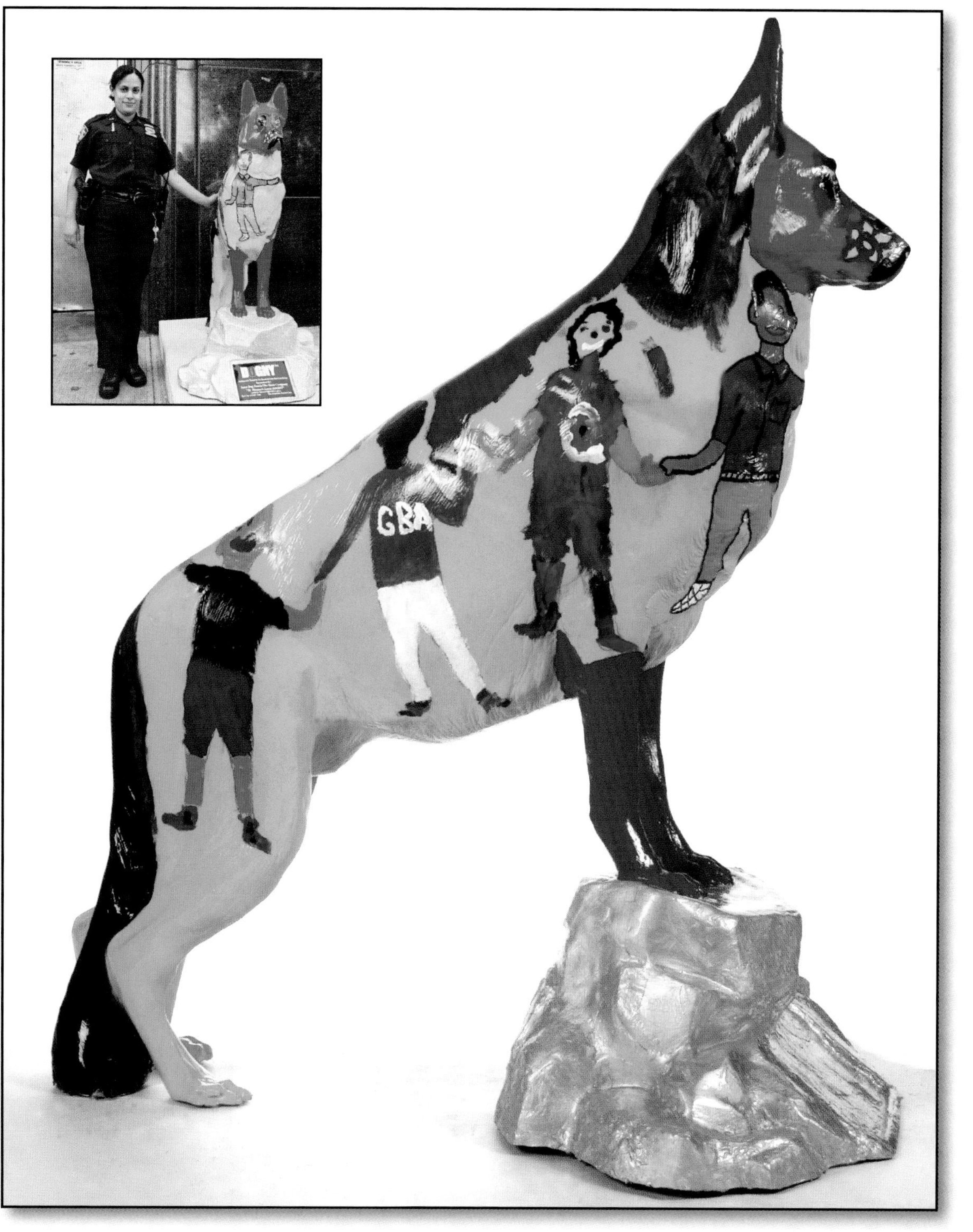

1983
DOGNY

DOGNY SM
AMERICA'S TRIBUTE TO SEARCH AND RESCUE DOGS
Sponsored By:
Bayer
"Natural German Shepherd Dog"
The City of New York
The American Kennel Club

Natural German Shepherd Dog

Christopher Jarrett

About the Artwork:

"When I was three, I fell into an irrigation ditch at my father's ranch in Tucson. Our trusted dog, Chief, was able to fetch my father and lead him to me moments before water chutes were to be opened, which surely would have resulted in my drowning. It was my privilege to be involved in honoring these wonderful creatures of God and friends to man."

About the Artist:

Christopher Jarrett was born in Tucson, Arizona. He has studied with a variety of artists—proponents of a broad spectrum of styles and methods—in Portland, Oregon, New York City and Brussels, Belgium. In the early 1970s, he was the artistic director of the experimental theater company "Proteus Mime Theatre." Mr. Jarrett is known particularly for his land-, sea-, and sky-scapes of eastern Long Island and the Oregon coastline. He is also recognized for his original use of marble dust plasters in the creation of unusual "art/furniture" pieces.

Subway Map Dog

AMERICAN KENNEL CLUB
AKC
INCORPORATED

Jolanta Pienczykowski and Stephen Lugo

About the Artwork:

"What would it be like to view the city through the eyes of a dog? Everyone has their favorite restaurants, places to hang out and meet people...why can't a dog have city favorites as well? Here, all of our pooch's best places are pointed out on a very recognizable map of New York City—the subway map!"

About the Artist:

Jolanta Pienczykowski is a native New Yorker. She has loved to draw ever since she can remember and continued her passion for art by attending the School of Visual Arts in Manhattan. She completed her Bachelors degree in graphic design with a minor in Computer Graphics in 1994. Jolanta is currently a Senior Artist/Creative Manager at Sure Fit, Inc., a home furnishings company.

Stephen Lugo is also a native New Yorker and has known Jolanta Pienczykowski for 20 years. Stephen has always drawn comic book characters, especially his favorite, Spiderman.

Wall Street Dog

Jolanta Pienczykowski and Stephen Lugo

About the Artwork:

"Here's a tribute to one of New York's favorite characters—the businessman! Over the past few decades, the businessman has been portrayed in books, movies, and in the news constantly. After 9/11, it's only appropriate to also pay tribute to the many businessmen and women we lost."

About the Artists:

Jolanta Pienczykowski is a native New Yorker. She has loved to draw ever since she can remember and continued her passion for art by attending the School of Visual Arts in Manhattan. She completed her Bachelors degree in graphic design with a minor in Computer Graphics in 1994. Jolanta is currently a Senior Artist/Creative Manager at Sure Fit, Inc., a home furnishings company.

Stephen Lugo is also a native New Yorker and has known Jolanta Pienczykowski for 20 years. Stephen has always drawn comic book characters, especially his favorite, Spiderman.

Celebrate Our NYC Heroes

Kristin Doney

About the Artwork:

"My design aims to highlight the rich tapestry that is New York City and concurrently recognize the heroic efforts of the search and rescue dogs at Ground Zero."

About the Artist:

Kristin Doney is an illustrator specializing in children's books. She co-wrote and illustrated a book inspired by former Mayor Rudolph Giuliani titled *What Will You Be?* Doney studied art at Syracuse University and presently lives in Greenwich Village.

All Breeds and Bones

Beata Szpura

About the Artwork:

"The all breeds and bones dog is covered with pictures of several breeds and the pattern of bones."

About the Artist:

"I have been working as an artist and illustrator in New York City for the past 17 years. My work has appeared in publications such as the *New York Times*, *The Washington Post*, *Cosmopolitan*, *The Wall Street Journal*, *Seventeen*, *McCall's*, *Barron's*, and *The New Yorker*. My holiday greeting cards were published by the Museum of Modern Art. I also paint and illustrate children's books and teach drawing and collage classes at Parsons School of Design. I used to have a dog, a Field Spaniel, whom I loved very much."

Sponsor: Eukanuba Dog Foods/The Iams Company

A Girl and Her Dog

Mary Fragapane

About the Artwork:

"The inspiration for this design is the bond between dogs and their owners. The design features a realistic dog face that blends into the night sky, and several whimsical images that depict the relationship of people and their dogs. Included throughout this design are lighthearted quotes pertaining to dogs and the place they hold in our lives. This piece is partly a tribute to my beloved dog that I lost just a few months ago."

About the Artist:

Mary Fragapane is an emerging artist known for her figurative paintings representing the beauty of the human spirit. Mary's life, like her art, pulses with creative energy, and she most recently had great success with a showing of her work at Kanvas in the heart of Manhattan's art district, Chelsea. She has shown her work on both coasts, and has been the only New York artist invited to participate in the Art for Life charity auction in San Francisco for the last three years. As a muralist, Mary has painted several large-scale murals for both private and public spaces and was one of the artists commissioned to paint for the Woodstock '99 commemorative peace wall, for which she designed and painted over 500 feet of murals.

Heart of Gold

AMERICAN KENNEL CLUB
A·K·C
INCORPORATED

Kerry Bonner

About the Artwork:

"When thinking about search and rescue dogs, so many emotions come to mind. They give a sense of hope and pride with their bravery and loyalty to those waiting for and watching them do their work. The dog that I designed is called 'Heart of Gold' because I am sure all rescue dogs must have one! It seems they only want to please, even if they are in danger. The design is for a German Shepherd Dog painted pretty realistically, with the exception of a heart of gold on his chest that is slightly raised in texture. Also, the rescue vest (which is painted on, not attached) has a poem written on the back to signify the importance of man's best friend and the amazing job they do to help us."

About the Artist:

"I am a traditional and digital illustrator. My style tends to be very decorative, hip, colorful, and eye-catching. My traditional art training started at Otis Parsons Art Institute in Los Angeles, then continued a few years later at the Academy of Art College in San Francisco, with an emphasis on computer graphics and animation."

Starry Night Dog

AMERICAN KENNEL CLUB INCORPORATED AKC

Kerry Bonner

About the Artwork:

"When thinking about search and rescue dogs, so many emotions come to mind. They give a sense of hope and pride with their bravery and loyalty to those waiting for and watching them do their work. We feel joy for the people they successfully rescue and feel heartache for those they can't help. When I am missing a loved one no longer with me, sometimes I look up to the sky and think of them up there as a star. That is why I chose to do my styled version of Van Gogh's *Starry Night*, but with New York as the setting."

About the Artist:

"I am a traditional and digital illustrator. My style tends to be very decorative, hip, colorful, and eye-catching. My traditional art training started at Otis Parsons Art Institute in Los Angeles, then continued a few years later at the Academy of Art College in San Francisco, with an emphasis on computer graphics and animation."

Our Melting Pot

Dave Alsobrooks

About the Artwork:

"With this design I attempted to simultaneously pay tribute to all of the people and dogs (victims and survivors) of the 9/11 attacks—to accentuate the human-canine bond. Many people and dogs of all shapes, sizes, and colors are represented on this dog sculpture. This reflects the diverse nature of the people and of the search and rescue dogs used at the World Trade Center site. The dog is white, symbolic of the search and rescue dog's willingness to sacrifice her/himself to help others. This dog has sacrificed any physical identity to become the vehicle for promoting the cause held up by the hands and paws painted on its surface."

About the Artist:

Dave Alsobrooks is primarily a painter, but he is interested in all kinds of art. He is an art director for an advertising agency. His current paintings, large abstracts, reflect his interest in color and texture. He is also interested in a variety of materials in his normal working process, including steel, plex, board, and canvas.

DOGNY

You Have Touched Our Hearts!

Robert L. Braun and Christopher Jarrett

About the Artwork:

This sculpture was created to honor the first-time responders and their purebred canine companions. . . You have touched our hearts! The wreath around the neck of this sculpture suggests that search and rescue dogs are all winners in the race to save human lives.

About the Artists:

World-renowned artist Robert Braun brings a mix of his personal commitment and passion for wildlife to his masterfully sculpted works of art. He studied art history and sculpting at the University of Di Breira in Milan, Italy. He then received his Masters degree at The London International Film School, where he studied live action and animation. Over the past 20 years, Mr. Braun has created animation, FX's, and artwork for books, museums, and the film industry.

Christopher Jarrett was born in Tucson, Arizona. He has studied with a variety of artists—proponents of a broad spectrum of styles and methods—in Portland, Oregon, New York City and Brussels, Belgium. In the early 1970s, he was the artistic director of the experimental theater company "Proteus Mime Theatre." Mr. Jarrett is known particularly for his land-, sea-, and sky-scapes of eastern Long Island and the Oregon coastline. He is also recognized for his original use of marble dust plasters in the creation of unusual "art/furniture" pieces.

K-9 Police

Robert L. Braun

About the Artwork:

"Sculptured vest over painted dog."

About the Artist:

World-renowned artist Robert Braun brings a mix of his personal commitment and passion for wildlife to his works of art. He studied art history and sculpting at the University of Di Breira in Milan, Italy. He then received his Masters degree at The London International Film School, where he studied live action and animation. Over the past 20 years, Mr. Braun has created animation, FX's, and artwork for books, museums, and the film industry. He specializes in robotics and sculpting.

Mr. Braun's sculptures are in numerous private collections, as well as The Museum of Scotland, The British Museum of Natural History, and the National Museum of Science, Taiwan.

Merry-Go-Hound

Roy Rivera

About the Artwork:

"I wanted to keep a light, uplifting feeling for this project. The proud stance of the dog lent itself nicely as a carousel figure. I tried to portray how rescue dogs carry us all with their determination and bravery in helping assist people in our lives. With his proud breastplate and red, white, and blue banner, we honor man's best friend. The small flowers below the front paws growing from the cracks in the rock express life rising up from the rubble."

About the Artist:

"Basically, I'm a doodler and a daydreamer, but I have studied art at Bergen Community College and the Art Students League in New York City. Traditionally an oil painter specializing in surrealism and trompe-l'oeil, I have also tried airbrushing, wood carving, fly tying, and customizing 1:64-scale diecast cars."

Freedom Begins with Me

Michael P. Rodriguez

About the Artwork:

"A lot of people do not realize how much a drill sergeant means to a soldier. The drill sergeant is an elite military soldier who trains others to follow in his footsteps. They are the very foundation of building today's Armed Forces, because without them, people would not know what to do or how to be a soldier. Soldiers in the Armed Forces fight for our freedom, and the drill sergeant teaches men and women how to be a soldier, which is why the design is titled as such. I am in the Army Reserves, and I love the man I have become. What inspired me to do the piece is the fact that I remember my drill sergeants. They help me understand what it means to be a soldier and how it feels to serve one's country. "

About the Artist:

"I love art, it relaxes me and lets me appreciate the life I live. I have done drawings and sculptures since I was eight years old at The Jefferson Park Boy's Club on 111th Street between First and Second Avenues. I sometimes go to my neighborhood to see some of the people who have inspired my art and me."

Day and Night

Sofia Gawer-Fische

About the Artwork:

"I want to emphasize how these tireless dogs are always ready 24 hours a day to help rescue people. The design gradually goes from day to night. On one side of the sculpture, I painted a beautiful blue sky with white clouds and a sun; on the other side of the sculpture, a nighttime dark blue sky, with a moon and stars."

About the Artist:

"I was born in Buenos Aires, Argentina, where I graduated from the Prilidiano Pueyrredón National School of Fine Arts, with two degrees as Professor of Printing/Engraving and as Professor of Sculptures/Drawings. I moved to Washington, D.C., in 1989. My art works were exhibited at the Fredericksburg Museum in Virginia, The Embassy of Argentina, the Pan American Health Organization, The US Botanical Garden, Mexican Cultural Institute, the Colonnade Gallery at George Washington University, and The Art Barn Gallery in Washington, D.C.

"I have been teaching bilingual art workshops at different sites in the Washington area, including The Corcoran Gallery of Art, The Art Museum of the Americas, The Washington International School, and The Sidwell Friends Lower School."

Sponsor: Iams Dog Foods/The Iams Company

Bone-A-Fide Hero

Gus Ramos

About the Artwork:

"Bone-A-Fide Hero was inspired by the bravery and efforts of both man and dog during the recovery and rescue operations of the 9/11 disaster. All fire and police personnel involved showed their selflessness and patriotism by devoting countless hours of service. Equally, search and rescue dogs also contributed their talents, sniffing and searching through the rubble in the effort to locate loved ones lost in the disaster, making them true patriots as well. Many accolades have been bestowed upon New York's finest and bravest. How would the dogs choose to be thanked for their heroism? They'd probably ask for a bone!"

About the Artist:

Gus Ramos is a local artist and textile designer. A graduate of the Fashion Institute of Technology in Manhattan, Mr. Ramos has done numerous works of art for charity and private projects.

Max: Midnight Sky

About the Artwork:

"Our German Shepherd just passed away this year, and I was really inspired to do a tribute to him. He was a love dog—loyal and eager to please. I hope he is in a place that is as comforting as he was. I absolutely love dogs and always wanted to get into training them. I truly appreciate their existence. Dogs have always been my favorite."

About the Artist:

"I graduated from the University of Tennessee with a BFA in Design and Illustration. I've been mainly doing Web and CD ROM design for the past several years, and I plan on going back to school to earn a Masters in Industrial Design."

AMERICA
FDNY

DOGNY SM
AMERICA'S TRIBUTE TO SEARCH AND RESCUE DOGS
Sponsored By:
Reckson Associates
"New York's Valor"
The City of New York
The American Kennel Club

New York's Valor

Charles Fazzino

About the Artwork:

A larger-than-life depiction of the search and rescue dog standing guard over a peaceful city in the wake of a terrible tragedy.

About the Artist:

Charles Fazzino's 3-D limited editions and original paintings are exhibited in more than 500 fine art galleries in 15 different countries. Most famous for his 3-D cityscapes, Fazzino has also had the privilege of creating work for the United States Olympic Committee, the NFL's Super Bowl, NBC's Today Show, and the Rosie O'Donnell Show, among others.

I Love NY Search and Rescue

Adrien Zap

About the Artwork:

"The inspiration for this design draws from the overwhelming resurgence in popularity of the 'I Love NY'* logo after the September 11, 2001 tragedy. This popular icon, incorporating a red heart and basic black text, became an endless source of pride and faith in New York City, New York State, and across America. This simple logo has come to symbolize the incredible unity that brought millions of people together, in spite of tragedy, in order to rebuild and heal."

About the Artist:

Adrien Zap is a sophomore at New York University, where she is majoring in photography.

**Note: The registered I LOVE NEW YORK logos are the property of the New York State Department of Economic Development. The NYS Department of Economic Development has granted Ms. Zap permission for her artwork as it appears here for the AKC DOGNY Application and for limited related non-profit uses.*

Iris' Irises

Peter Soriano with Francesca Soriano

About the Artwork:

"My sculpture is first and foremost an homage to Iris Love. I wanted to merge together her two passions, Dachshunds and classical Greek culture. Happily united in the very appropriate meaning of her name, Iris (the messenger of the gods), these Dachshunds wander and play between a most un-Olympian temple and our beloved New York. I must also mention my collaborator, my daughter, Francesca Soriano, and our four-legged muse, Amalthea."

About the Artist:

Peter Soriano is a sculptor who exhibits regularly in the US and Europe. He attended the Skowhegan School of Art in Maine before moving to New York. He now teaches sculpture at the School of Visual Arts and is represented by the Lennon Weinberg gallery. His work has been collected by institutions such as Fogg Art Museum in Massachusetts and the Cartier Foundation in Paris.

Sponsor: In honor of Professor Iris Cornelia Love from Anne Radice

Sammy—Uncle Sam's Dog

Colleen Corradi

About the Artwork:

This rendition of an American icon is highlighted with a top hat, hair, beard and suit. It portrays the bond that has kept dogs and people working together throughout our country's history.

About the Artist:

"After earning a degree in languages and a diploma in fine art, I started travelling and attending specialized art courses in London, Oklahoma City, and finally New York, where I attended the Art Student's League. I took my art one step further by joining Bob Blackburn's Studio, working among professional printmakers. I have extensively worked in the printmaking area, although my background studies as a painter and sculptor always come up in my artwork. I am currently working on a project based on the theme of war, which depicts people's feelings, rather than the actual facts."

Natural German Shepherd

Robert L. Braun

About the Artwork:

"Painted in natural colors with realistic Shepherd glass eyes."

About the Artist:

World-renowned artist Robert Braun brings a mix of his personal commitment and passion for wildlife to his masterfully sculpted works of art.

Mr. Braun studied art history and sculpting at the University of Di Breira in Milan, Italy. He then received his Masters degree at The London International Film School, where he studied live action and animation. Over the past 20 years, Mr. Braun has created animation, FX's, and artwork for books, museums, and the film industry. He specializes in robotics and sculpting.

Mr. Braun's sculptures are in numerous private collections, as well as The Museum of Scotland, The British Museum of Natural History, and the National Museum of Science, Taiwan.

Caught in the Search

Sharon Moore Gallery

About the Artwork:

"The design was an inspiration I had after a conversation with some friends. Our idea was to use all the names of all of all the victims from September 11. Our dog looks like a real dog from a distance, but as you get closer to the statue, you can read the names of all of the victims. We made the face and paws realistic, then they fade into the names, which were applied in the way that hair grows on a dog."

About the Artists:

"I own an art gallery and am privileged to represent many local artists. I invited two of them to assist me with this project. We decided to go under the name of the gallery, but here is the individual information:

Susan Wright—Resident of Telford, PA.
Fine Arts teacher at Souderton High School.
Nicholas Pugliese—Resident of Lansdale, PA.
Artist and employee of Sharon Moore Gallery
Sharon Lynn Moore—Resident of Souderton, PA.
Artist and owner of Sharon Moore Gallery.
Dr. Sharon and Jim Minninger—Telford Veterinary Hospital.
Gary Soden—Resident of Telford, PA."

Brave New World

Mary Fragapane

About the Artwork:

"This design is inspired by the tragic events of September 11 and the resounding sense of patriotism that keeps our country united. It features a backdrop of the American flag. In the foreground is the New York skyline, with the Chrysler and Empire State buildings and the Statue of Liberty, as well as the wreckage at Ground Zero, with detail of rescue dogs at work with their handlers."

About the Artist:

Mary Fragapane is an emerging artist known for her figurative paintings representing the beauty of the human spirit. She most recently showed her work at Kanvas in the heart of Manhattan's art district, Chelsea. She has shown her work on both coasts, and has been the only New York artist invited to participate in the Art for Life charity auction in San Francisco for the last three years. As a muralist, Mary has painted several large-scale murals for both private and public spaces and was one of the artists commissioned to paint for the Woodstock '99 commemorative peace wall, for which she designed and painted over 500 feet of murals.

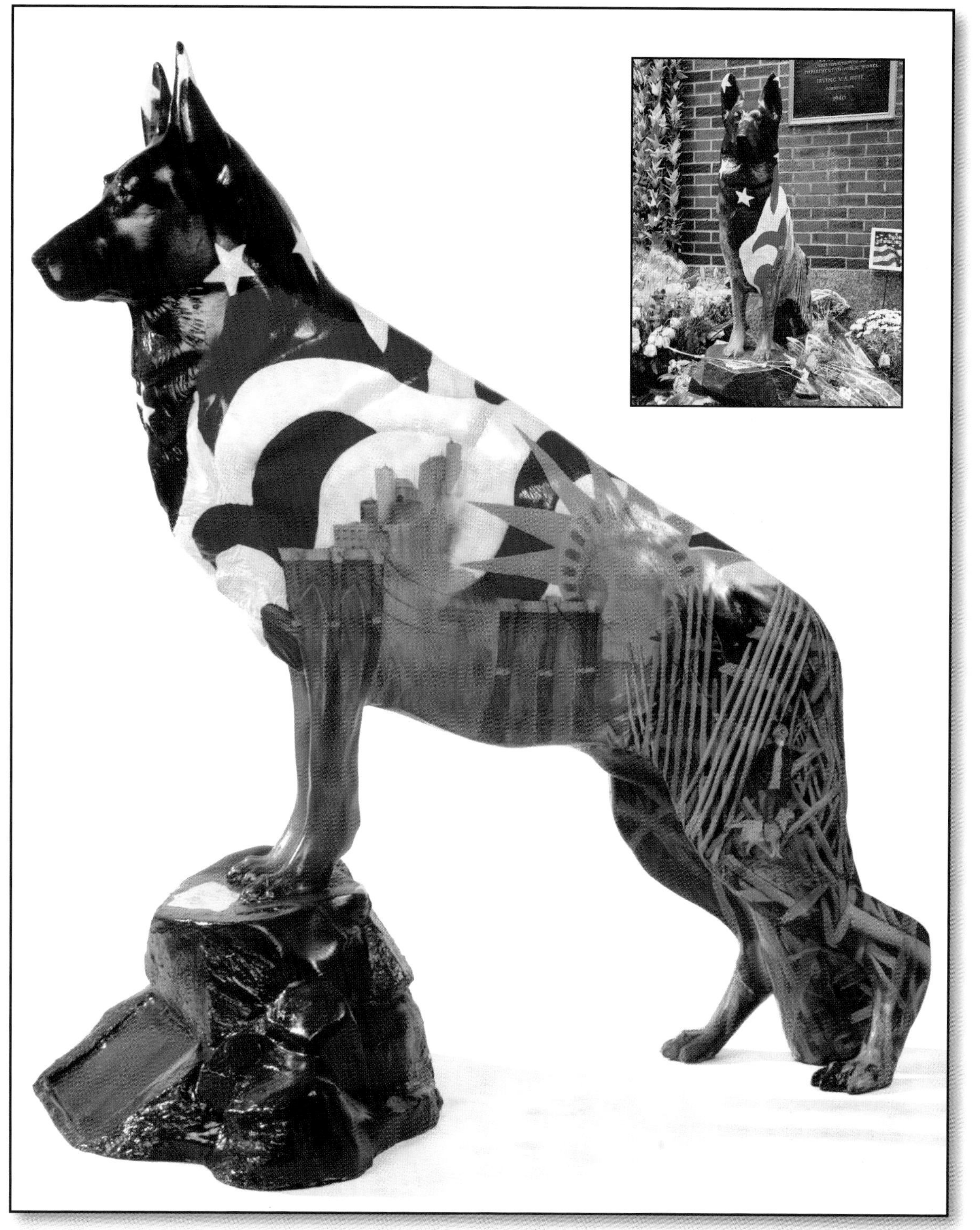

Sponsor: Pfizer Animal Health Group

NYC Search and Rescue Police Dog

Michael Cuomo

About the Artwork:

"Two chrome towers are painted on each side of the dog's uniform. A badge with NYPD in blue and chrome is painted on the chest with NYPD and #9. Real black booties are bonded on each paw in black. A police cap is bonded to dog's head, and a full police uniform is painted on the body. Representing collapse, heavy chrome and black are on the bottom of the uniform. The rest of the uniform is covered in wire and metal paint."

About the Artist:

"Prior to 9/11, I was never consciously patriotic, but being in New York City and living in the shocking reality of that day, I arose to a different plateau of awareness. Previously unimportant symbols became important—the flag, our country, and my city. My new works include past methods of expression and new unknown values. Earlier projects were more sculptural in nature, including construction and woodworking, and it seemed natural to bring these techniques into my new works."

Liberty's Light

Susan Jacob

About the Artwork:

"This design was inspired by the votive candles that were constantly kept lit and on display after September 11, 2001. This reminded me of Lady Liberty, and I envisioned her holding a special votive toward her neighbors, the Twin Towers—both such distinct symbols of New York City and of the United States of America. Her vigilance has been echoed by the incredible rescue teams who worked non-stop to recover victims from September 11, 2001, and on innumerable other occasions."

About the Artist:

"I always had access to paint, and at about the same time I started to show dogs, my art became serious. So, throughout high school I filled my curriculum with art courses and entered many competitions. I received a Gold Key Scholastic Art Award in painting in 2000, a Silver Key in Sculpture in 1996, and Honorable Mentions in painting in 1998 and 1999. I also have published artwork in the *AKC Gazette*. I continue to explore my range as a visual artist even while attending North Carolina School of the Arts, School of Filmmaking."

Galaxy Dog

Robert L. Braun

About the Artwork:

"A view of our galaxy."

About the Artist:

World-renowned artist Robert Braun brings a mix of his personal commitment and passion for wildlife to his works of art. He studied art history and sculpting at the University of Di Breira in Milan, Italy. He then received his Masters degree at The London International Film School, where he studied live action and animation. Over the past 20 years, Mr. Braun has created animation, FX's, and artwork for books, museums, and the film industry.

Mr. Braun's sculptures are in numerous private collections, as well as The Museum of Scotland, The British Museum of Natural History, and the National Museum of Science, Taiwan.

Magritte Dog

Beata Szpura

About the Artwork:

"The Magritte dog is inspired by the surreal landscapes of the painter René Magritte."

About the Artist:

"I have been working as an artist and illustrator in New York City for the past 17 years. My work has appeared in publications such as *The New York Times, The Washington Post, Cosmopolitan, The Wall Street Journal, Seventeen, McCall's, Barron's,* and *The New Yorker*. My holiday greeting cards were published by the Museum of Modern Art. I also paint and illustrate children's books and teach drawing and collage classes at Parsons School of Design. I used to have a dog, a Field Spaniel, whom I loved very much."

Sponsor: The Petco Foundation and The Iams Company •

Doggy Dog

AMERICAN KENNEL CLUB INCORPORATED AKC

Beata Szpura

About the Artwork:

"Doggy Dog is covered with happy faces of dogs of different breeds, as well as mutts."

About the Artist:

"I have been working as an artist and illustrator in New York City for the past 17 years. My work has appeared in publications such as the *New York Times*, *The Washington Post*, *Cosmopolitan*, *The Wall Street Journal*, *Seventeen*, *McCall's*, *Barron's*, and *The New Yorker*. My holiday greeting cards were published by the Museum of Modern Art. I also paint and illustrate children's books and teach drawing and collage classes at Parsons School of Design. I used to have a dog, a Field Spaniel, whom I loved very much."

New York Pride

Billy

About the Artwork:

"New York Pride is simple: Miss Liberty and the fireman on one side; on the other side a policeman and a rescue worker. All those people, with the rescue dogs, are what we are so grateful and proud of—New York Pride."

About the Artist:

"Create Your Own Reality" is the mantra that Billy lives by. This self-taught East Village artist was recently featured in a half-page article in the *New York Times* profiling his life. Billy has exhibited his work in New York, Chicago, Cleveland and Austin, Texas. His list of corporate clients includes the Manhattan Jewish Community Center, Epic Records, Columbia Pictures, Spike Lee/Pizza Hut, and Sara Lee/Chock Full O' Nuts. Billy's mural projects have taken him all over the globe in the form of installations for such notable clients as DOGNY; Cow Parade New York and Las Vegas; Woodstock 99, where Billy designed and painted 2500 feet of murals for the "Peace Wall" surrounding the concert; the backdrop for the "Emerging Artist" stage; and the Broadway and London productions of *Rent*.

NEW YORK
HARRISON J. GOLDIN
COMPTROLLER

THE CITY OF

Robert L. Braun

About the Artwork:

"This sculpture is a relief on a large eagle head so as to minimize distortion when looking at the profile. The design and painting conform to the contour of the dog. The rubble is painted like natural cement and rock."

About the Artist:

World-renowned artist Robert Braun brings a mix of his personal commitment and passion for wildlife to his masterfully sculpted works of art. He studied art history and sculpting at the University of Di Breira in Milan, Italy. He then received his Masters degree at The London International Film School, where he studied live action and animation. Over the past 20 years, Mr. Braun has created animation, FX's, and artwork for books, museums, and the film industry. He specializes in robotics and sculpting. Mr. Braun's sculptures are in numerous private collections, as well as The Museum of Scotland, The British Museum of Natural History, and the National Museum of Science, Taiwan.

Sunshine and Daisies

Cindy Lass

About the Artwork:

"My dog is about nature, energy, and going back to being spiritual. The message is 'Keep life simple: Dogs, love, and nature.' Dogs and nature give an unconditional love and goodness. Life is wonderful energy, like dogs, sunshine, and beautiful things!"

About the Artist:

Cindy Lass is an acclaimed British artist who loves dogs. Cindy first achieved success as a film and television actress and dedicated herself to painting in 1994. Her work has been sold worldwide, and many celebrities own portraits of their pets painted by Cindy Lass.

Faces of the World

Jimm Carroll

About the Artwork:

"No two people have the same face. These individuals are what I call a gift of life. Not unlike the colors of the spectrum and each with its own beauty, strength, and grace. All of equal value—all precious."

About the Artist:

"I have been a commercial artist for over 20 years. After attending Parsons School of Design, I apprenticed with an architectural illustrator for 10 years. Thereafter, I began my own independent pursuits, which have ranged from advertising illustration to interior design to architecture. I also teach perspective drawing and architectural drawing techniques at a local college. None of my work is computer generated; it is all created organically with my head, my heart, and my hands."

Sponsor: Friends of The American Kennel Club

Rushing to the Rescue

Claudia Nagy

About the Artwork:

"This rescue dog is designed with gold leaf for the body, leather straps for the wings, carved/cutout wooden wings, and heavy rope. Pure as untarnished gold, with techno wings and equipment, this sculpture represents the unlimited love and willingness to sacrifice with fidelity. Transcending the limits of its own body, the generous rescue dog carries the hope to save."

About the Artist:

"I have studied and practiced fine arts since 1970, exhibited in several shows and won competitions in drawings and paintings. Since 1984, I have immersed myself in arts and crafts, using mostly stone, wood, and glass. In the last three years, I have been working with mosaics on flat and 3-D objects. I have participated in multiple shows in New York City, San Francisco, and Europe. I have done several commissions of murals and objects."

Majesty

Francine Iannelli

About the Artwork:

"This work was inspired by The National Ethnic Coalition of Organizations (NECO)'s recognition of diversity and how it makes our country great. Its rainbow of colors represents the variety of races and their blending into one, with the hope of world peace. These brave and dedicated American canine heroes perform their duties without prejudice or bias. These are the same qualities NECO represents."

About the Artist:

"I am an amateur artist who is studying Fine Arts as a part-time student. I am currently working as an associate event coordinator with the National Ethnic Coalition of Organizations."

Sponsor: Friends of The American Kennel Club

Aurora : Angel of Rescue

Robert Perless

About the Artwork:

"The cooperative relationship between humans and dogs has been a cornerstone of civilization. As civilization becomes more urban and complex, the relationship has changed significantly. Our four-legged partners have had to adapt and bring their extraordinary abilities to bear on a whole new set of circumstances.

"Aurora is my vision of the angel of rescue—visually energized, with the light surrounding it being transmuted into a rainbow. Its power radiates the energy of the sun, projecting rainbows throughout the environment."

About the Artist:

Robert Perless was born in Brooklyn, New York. He grew up across the street from Sheepshead Bay, where he began a lifelong fascination with sailing, fishing, and the life of the sea. He attended Cheshire Academy and the University of Miami in Florida, where he studied Art and Engineering.

Liberty

Lauren P. Mellusi

About the Artwork:

"At first glance, the viewer sees the statue draped from head to toe with our country's flag. The flag is waving in the wind to give the static sculpture grace, fluidity, and movement. From the side, the viewer is greeted by our lovely Lady Liberty, our most basic and ever-enduring symbol of freedom. She is painted with her fiery torch stretching high and burning bright. One side of the dog shows our beloved Twin Towers, the opposite side shows the illuminated Towers of Light."

About the Artist:

"Artistically, I have worked in various media, such as sculpture, drawing, and painting of still life and reproduction/imitation of famous works. I am also a co-art director and a volunteer with a local Girl Scout troop, where I teach arts and crafts and basic drawing techniques."

GOD BLESS AMERICA

New York Remembers

Charles Fazzino

About the Artwork:

This sculpture literally transforms our memories of 9/11 into 3-D art. The search and rescue dog keeps solemn watch over the World Trade Center, as loving citizens pay tribute to the New York City Police Department, the New York City Fire Department, and the New York City Port Authority Police Department.

About the Artist:

Charles Fazzino's 3-D limited editions and original paintings are exhibited in more than 500 fine art galleries in 15 different countries. Most famous for his 3-D cityscapes, Fazzino has also had the privilege of creating work for the United States Olympic Committee, the NFL's Super Bowl, NBC's Today Show, and the Rosie O'Donnell Show.

The Eyes of Hope... The Heart of a Hero

Nicholas Vito Macchio

About the Artwork:

"This sculpture is painted to look realistic—a German Shepherd with appropriate harness, with the eyes illuminated. It is an honor to pay tribute to the canine heroes that teach us more about humanity."

About the Artist:

Born in the Hells Kitchen district of New York City, Nicholas V. Macchio was raised in an artistic Italian/Greek family.

After graduating from college with a degree in Advertising Art & Design, Nicholas accepted a position as assistant art director for a major magazine. After some time, however, he discovered artistic happiness in freelance work and opted to work independently. It was during this period that he became involved in the animal rights movement. For over nine years, he volunteered his services and artistic capabilities to this cause, creating and donating all artwork (posters, paintings, newsletters, banners, etc.).

Dogwood

Dennis Eisenberg

About the Artwork:

"Dogs have always brought me a great deal of enjoyment. I wanted to bring as much joy as I could to my designs and the people who view them. I thought a good way to raise awareness would be to create a design that is bold, eye-catching, and perhaps clever in some way so it stands out wherever it's located."

About the Artist:

"I was a magazine art director and fine artist for many years and have been designing and building scenery for the theater for the past eight years."

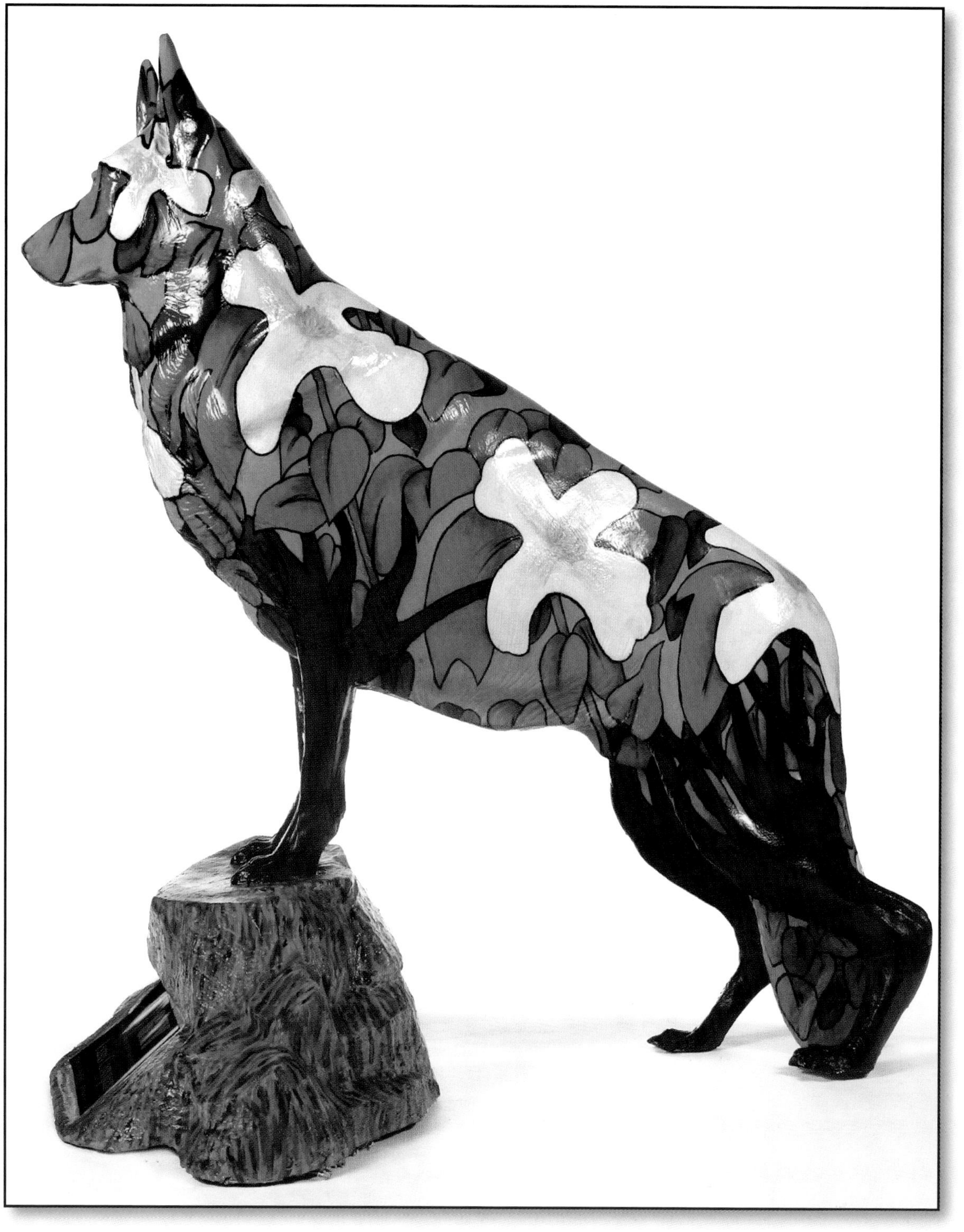

Sponsor: Amy Kiell and Harvey Schwartz, Pebbles' Run Samoyeds

Wooftop Rescue

Paul Farinacci

About the Artwork:

"I am in awe of the work done by these loyal creatures. Therefore, my design illustrates a fictitious recovery story involving the rescue of a small girl by a dog. The scene takes place on top of and inside the brick doghouse, with a fireman and the rescue dog on the back of the statue. The fearless canine crusader leads the way down the rescue ladder through an opening. Inside the structure, he locates the girl in need and escorts her to safety."

About the Artist:

Paul Farinacci has exhibited extensively and won many awards. He recently completed a cow sculpture for CowParade London in England.

 Sponsor: Ellen M. Charles and Melissa Cantacuzène, in memory of Adelaide Close Riggs

Rising

Lucia Yee-Lipitz

About the Artwork:

"The rescue dogs are proud, brave and resilient—a mirror of the city they helped after the attack of September 11. It is these common traits of dog and city that I wish to depict here. The image of the New York City skyline is based on a painting I exhibited at the Society of Illustrators last January. The show was created as an outlet for artists to express their emotions after the terrorist attack. The loose circular streak around the body of the dog symbolizes the island of Manhattan. On each side of the dog's body are different impressions of the city skyline: One side is cool and reflective, with blues, white, and black, while the other side is warm and hopeful, with a palate of white, yellow, orange, and red."

About the Artist:

"I am currently a textile artist at Polo/Ralph Lauren. My work has been exhibited in such galleries as the National Arts Club in Gramercy Park, the Society of Illustrators, the Arsenal Gallery, and Pelham Art Center. Last year I designed a 50-foot mural for the East Harlem School, which appeared in *Oprah Magazine*, and four murals of teddy bears in city settings that are permanently installed at the Ronald McDonald House."

Show Stoppers

Billy

About the Artwork:

"This design represents the energy and vitality of New York and the Broadway community—specifically shows and characters from the various Shubert Theaters on Broadway. From the disco-laced woman of *Mamma Mia* to the well-known image of the *Phantom of the Opera* mask, this dog is pure New York and Broadway."

About the Artist:

"Create Your Own Reality" is the mantra that Billy lives by. This self-taught East Village artist was recently featured in a half-page article in the *New York Times* profiling his life. Billy has exhibited his work in New York, Chicago, Cleveland, and Austin, Texas. His list of corporate clients includes the Manhattan Jewish Community Center, Epic Records, Columbia Pictures, Spike Lee/Pizza Hut, and Sara Lee/Chock Full O' Nuts. Billy's mural projects have taken him all over the globe in the form of installations for such notable clients as DOGNY; Cow Parade New York and Las Vegas; Woodstock 99, where Billy designed and painted 2500 feet of murals for the "Peace Wall" surrounding the concert; the backdrop for the "Emerging Artists" stage; and the Broadway and London productions of *Rent.*

Thinking About History

Evagelia Maravelias

About the Artwork:

"I, like many others, lost a loved one in the World Trade Center disaster. I was living in New York at the time of the tragedy and watched in shock as everything unfolded. I was glad to be able to give thanks in my own way, offering a personal tribute through my craft for this very special project. It depicts the dog viewing framed images of American symbols: the eagle, stars and stripes, etc. As viewers looking at art, we are looking at a template of time. In this moment we are living the past, even for a brief second, through the depiction of the artist. We are forced to place ourselves in time, becoming and experiencing a part of history."

About the Artist:

"I am an artist who currently focuses on human landscapes, both physical and psychological. Whether it is fantasy, reality, or the recollection of childhood memory, visual language is layered and mixed with personal iconography that abstracts the human anatomy. Environments that resonate initial safety prove volatile upon closer inspection."

Dog Love Power

Manjusha Shandler

About the Artwork:

"In my work, my aim is to capture the heart-love-soul-essence of dogs' noble beings."

About the Artist:

"I have been specialized for years in painting portraits of dogs. Since graduating from Bard College, I have shown my work in New York, New Jersey, and California. I teach drawing and painting to children and adults and conduct creativity workshops coaching people to re-connect to their authentic, creative selves."

One

Allison Aboud

About the Artwork:

"My DOGNY design is a dedication to the service animals who risked their lives to help bring order to the pandemonium of the New York City and Washington, DC terrorist attacks. The design depicts this transition from disorder to order using a painting technique reminiscent of cubism."

About the Artist:

Allison Aboud is an artist from the Washington, DC area. She has a deep love for animals, especially dogs, and volunteered for several years at the Humane Society in New Hampshire and Washington, DC. A graduate of Dartmouth College, she will be attending American University for a Master of Fine Arts program in painting.

Let Freedom Ring

Kathryn Mellusi

About the Artwork:

"Inspiration for this piece stems primarily from the aftermath of 9-11. In order to help our country maintain a strong sense of pride, this patriotic theme is proudly and aerodynamically designed with strength, movement, and fluidity. Elements of the Twin Towers, Liberty torch, American bald eagle, and flag are incorporated in such a way that all 'panels' of the entire dog are unified into one gracefully fluid and windblown structure. A small red heart inscribed with the word 'Love' can be found in the front center of the ribbon directly between the eagle's talons. Love, then, becomes the mural's central core from which all other elements flow and are tied into by the ribbon. It is the key factor that unifies the piece."

About the Artist:

"I am a 25-year-old artist born and raised in the Bronx. I graduated from Binghamton University and attend Brooklyn Law School. I am working for the Bronx District Attorney's office and hope to get a job as a special agent in the FBI. Although art is not a career for me, it has been my saving grace."

Superman's Best Friend

Paul Bianca

About the Artwork:

Paul Bianca instantly recognized the correlation between the heroism of the search and rescue dogs and the comic book superheroes, such as Captain America and others. His superhero search and rescue dog in his design represents the innate ability of all dogs to be heroic in the face of danger, in particular when helping those in need of rescue. As opposed to superheroes, who are unusually brave and heroic, these dogs are all natural heroes.

About the Artist:

Paul Bianca is Brooklyn-born and based, and was schooled in illustration and painting at the High School of Art & Design. He's been illustrating professionally in New York City for 20 years. His style is most influenced by the illustrations of Jack Kirby of early Marvel superhero comics.

Sponsor: Bollinger Insurance and The Chubb Group of Insurance Companies

 • *Sponsor: Petco and The Iams Company*

Police Athletic League Loves DOGNY

Luis Vargas

About the Artwork:

The PAL Loves DOGNY sculpture was painted by the winner of the Police Athletic League/IAMS art contest, Luis Vargas, age 13. Following the announcement by New York Police Commissioner Ray Kelly, Luis's rendering of a New York City skyline, highlighting the Twin Towers, was painted at PAL's Carnival Day in Central Park.

About the Artist and the Police Athletic League

"Although it was difficult to choose just one drawing out of the over 200 submissions by the children of the PAL summer programs, Luis Vargas was a clear winner with all the judges," said Commissioner Ray Kelly.

Founded in 1914, the Police Athletic League (PAL) is one of the largest non-profit youth agencies in New York City. PAL provides 65,000 children with the opportunities they need to lead meaningful and productive lives.

In Dog We Trust

Ron Burns

About the Artwork:

"In Dog We Trust" brings a rush of color and warmth to DOGNY. In this sculpture, a dog finds himself at home on an overstuffed armchair in a cozy, bright living room. This piece suggests that no home is complete without a faithful dog as a loving member of the family.

About the Artist:

Ron Burns has the distinction of being the first and only Artist In Residence for the Humane Society of the United States and is the Official Artist for the ASPCA's Adopt a Shelter Dog Month, 2001 and 2002.

K-9 Ladder

Paul Farinacci

About the Artwork:

"I have always been concerned with childhood memories and social commentary in my work. One in particular involves an innocent child re-enacting the attacks on the World Trade Center while playing with blocks and toy cars, trucks, and planes. An old metal toy fire engine included in this work ultimately became the initial inspiration for my Ladder Company K-9 dog design.

"My design involves the coming together of a living being and a mechanical device. It incorporates parts from a real toy fire engine. Its body is painted to resemble a fire truck in a palette of red, white, silver, and black. His head is still all canine, with the exception of his firefighter hat.

"This design is also in response to all the selfless acts and collaborations made by the search and rescue dogs and the firefighters, as well as other emergency service workers at the World Trade Center. I chose the symbol of the fire truck because dogs and the fire department have always had a special kind of bond."

About the Artist:

Paul Farinacci has exhibited extensively and won many awards. He recently completed a cow sculpture for CowParade London in England.

Sponsor: Mr. & Mrs. Roger Rechler

Comic Strip Canine

Syd Hap

About the Artwork:

"I have always believed that art is a catalyst for change. This belief has motivated my use of art-making to facilitate problem solving and self-actualization with people through workshops and individual sessions."

About the Artist:

Syd Hap is a doll sculptor and a mixed media artist. For 15 years, she has been a master sculptor for Betty Boop, Popeye, and other King Features characters for product manufacturers nationwide. Syd also works with children and adults in her New York City studio utilizing art-making for personal growth.

The Precision of a Dog's Heart

Mary Ann Paredes

About the Artwork:

"The dog, presented in full color, is my interpretation of the many photos and accounts of the rescue dogs' mission. It is drawn in panoramic style to evoke the endless struggle that these teams of dogs went through as they searched for any sign of life and recovered the scent of any human remains. The scenes express stylistically the emotion and devastation while continuing to be hopeful. The style of painting is an expression of the mood set by the scene."

About the Artist:

"I would be lying if I said something profound about my art. I like to paint things that I am familiar with. I suppose that you could say I paint relationships I have with people, things, and events in my life that I believe should only be interesting (truthfully) to me. My style is pretty straightforward. I paint so you know what it is, I like playing with color and texture, and I like to concern myself with composition and design. I think everyone lies almost all the time and since I'm part of everyone, I try to not lie in one aspect of my life. This is the part I share with an audience, and the irony of it is that to tell the truth, I had to be completely quiet."

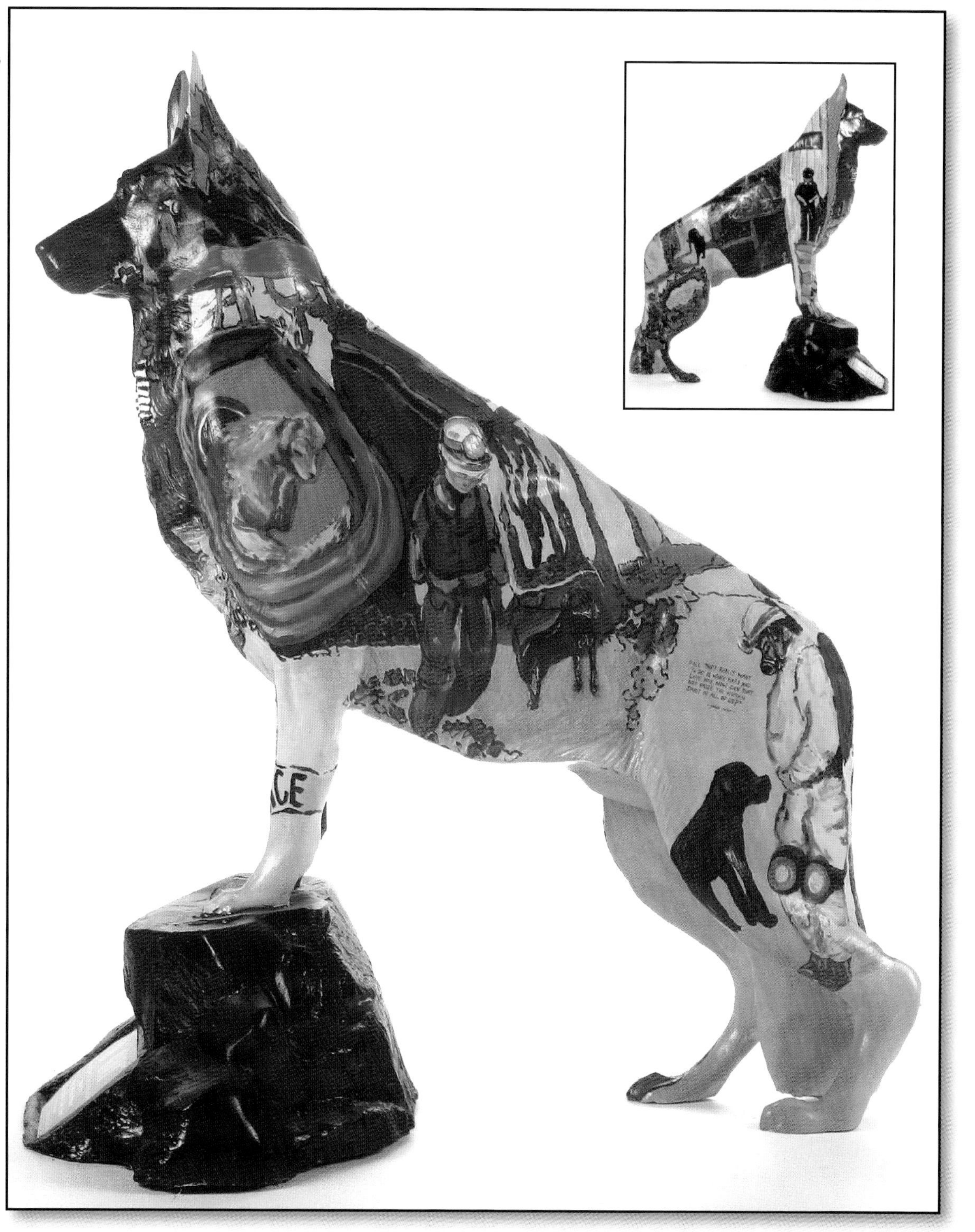

Sponsor: Corey and Alicia Pinkston

American Pedigree

AMERICAN KENNEL CLUB
A·K·C
INCORPORATED

Winifred S. DeWitt

About the Artwork:

"This design is simple. The red, white, and blue banner blankets the noble German Shepherd rescue dog with the canine's own attributes—bravery, strength, honor, and faithfulness."

About the Artist:

Born and raised in northeastern Pennsylvania, W.S. DeWitt holds the fine art positions of sculptor, model maker, wax chaser, and painter. With her years of experience working in the wax department of Joel Meisner & Co., Inc., (now known as Elliot Gantz & Co., Inc.), a bronze casting foundry in Farmingdale, New York, she has gone on to include among her skills and talents the completion of a number of finished bronze sculptures via commissions for private collections; the enlargement or reduction of existing sculptures for notable artists; model making using media such as clay, foam, plaster, and spackling in preparation for bronze casting; and the reconstruction and repair of damaged sculptures for various clients. Her educational background includes Keystone Junior College, The Art Institute of Fort Lauderdale, FL, and Parsons School of Design, NY.

Bahama Dog

Mark Schofield

About the Artwork:

"Tommy Bahama, the apparel company sponsoring the dog I painted, has a motto: 'Purveyors of Island Lifestyles.' Tropicana, being one of their many themes, is the direction I chose for this project, with its wide variety of imagery to draw from."

About the Artist:

"I've lived in Seattle, Washington, since 1990, employed as an artist on a freelance, project-by-project basis. Clients have included graphic design firms, restaurants, festival producers, apparel companies, corporations, magazines, books, and illustrations for exhibits."

News Hound

Lois Weiss and Mona Weiss

About the Artwork:

"Rescue dogs are often lauded in the press, and our News Hound has sniffed out appropriate headlines and articles that are being worn as an artistic collage celebrating all K-9 corps heroics. His piece contains actual newspaper clippings celebrating the heroic dogs arranged into a collage directly on the sculpture."

About the Artists:

This mother-daughter team of artists and visionaries is composed of two generations of talented dog lovers.

Lois Weiss is a writer and photographer whose work has appeared in publications including the *New York Post*, the *New York Times* and the *Robb Report*, and been displayed in the Washington Square Art Show. She has always loved dogs and is president of the local nature center.

Mona Weiss is a 19-year-old Hampshire College student and accomplished artist whose work has appeared in galleries and shows throughout Westchester and in Soho. She enjoys working in air-brush, mixed media, and collage. She inherited her love of animals from her mother and is particularly interested in animal behavior and rehabilitation.

Sirius

Allison Aboud

About the Artwork:

"My DOGNY design is a dedication to the service animals who risked their lives to help bring order to the pandemonium of the New York City and Washington, D.C. terrorist attacks. The design depicts this transition from disorder to order using a painting technique reminiscent of cubism. The top area of the dog (near the head) portrays a peaceful nighttime skyline in contrast to the disarray at the bottom lower half of the statue. The area of order and calm is painted between the head and heart of the service dog, because it is from the combined effort of the animal's intellect and loving nature that families with missing loved ones may find answers, security, and peace."

About the Artist:

Allison Aboud is an artist from the Washington, D.C. area. She has a deep love for animals, especially dogs, and volunteered for several years at the Humane Society in New Hampshire and Washington, D.C. A graduate of Dartmouth College, she will be attending American University for a Master of Fine Arts program in painting.

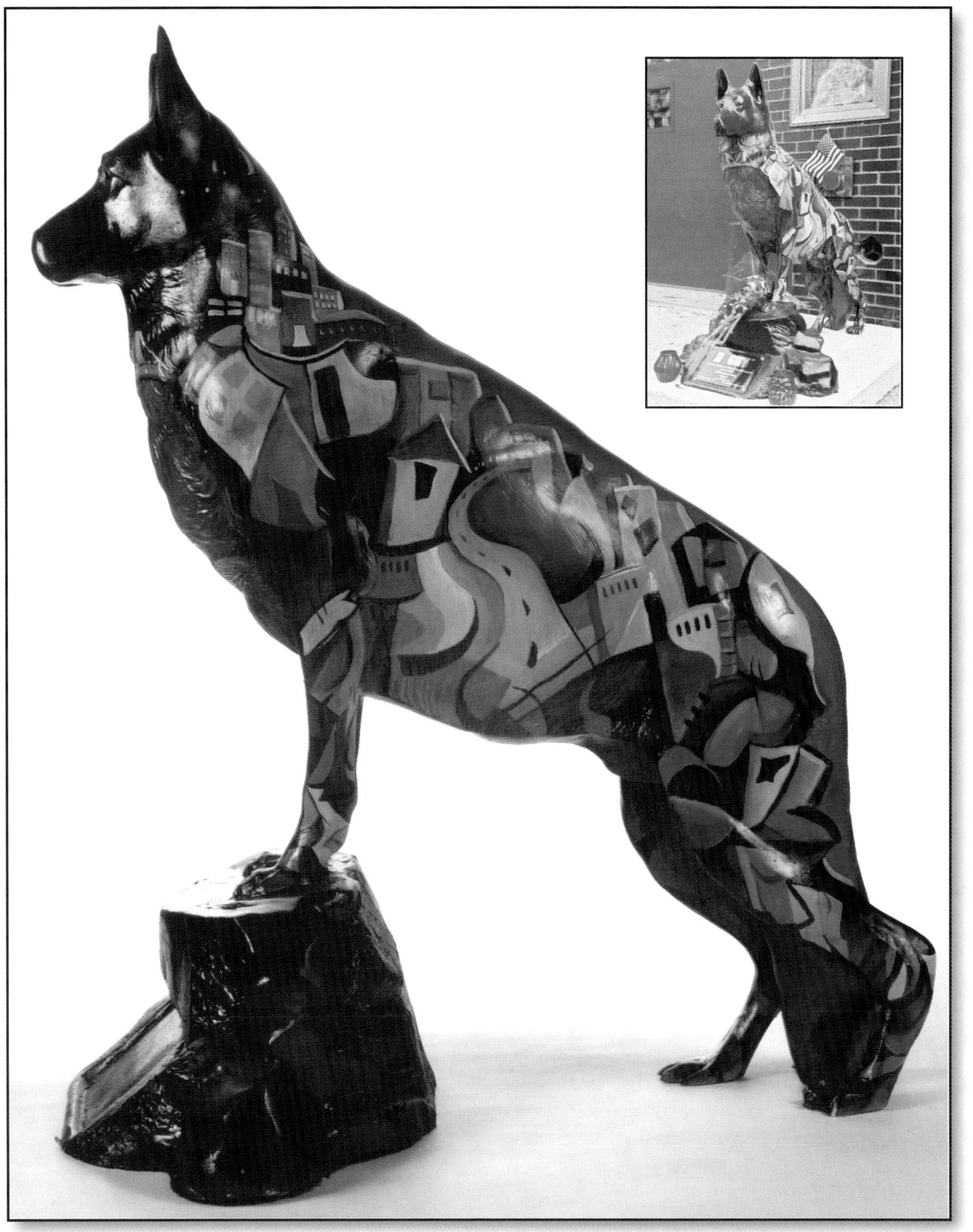

Bone-A-Fide Patriot

Gus Ramos

About the Artwork:

Bone-A-Fide Patriot was inspired by his first sculpture, Bone-A-Fide Hero. (see page 44)

About the Artist:

Gus Ramos is a local artist and textile designer. A graduate of the Fashion Institute of Technology in Manhattan, Mr. Ramos has done numerous works of art for charity and private projects.

The Strength of Our Rope

Kathryn Mellusi

About the Artwork:

"This moving and powerful piece symbolically depicts all forces that banded together in New York City on September 11 to aid in the relief and recovery efforts on that fateful day and to pay tribute to America's search and rescue dogs.

"Using the simple concept of a golden rope, this piece portrays both human and divine forces that were heavily relied upon for courage, strength, and hope in such a tragic time of need. Rescue workers, angels, and even higher celestial signs are all tied into the rope and work together to attain a common goal—to save the City of New York."

About the Artist:

"I am a 25-year-old artist born and raised in the Bronx. I graduated from Binghamton University and attend Brooklyn Law School. I am working for the Bronx District Attorney's office and hope to get a job as a special agent in the FBI. Although art is not a career for me, it has been my saving grace."

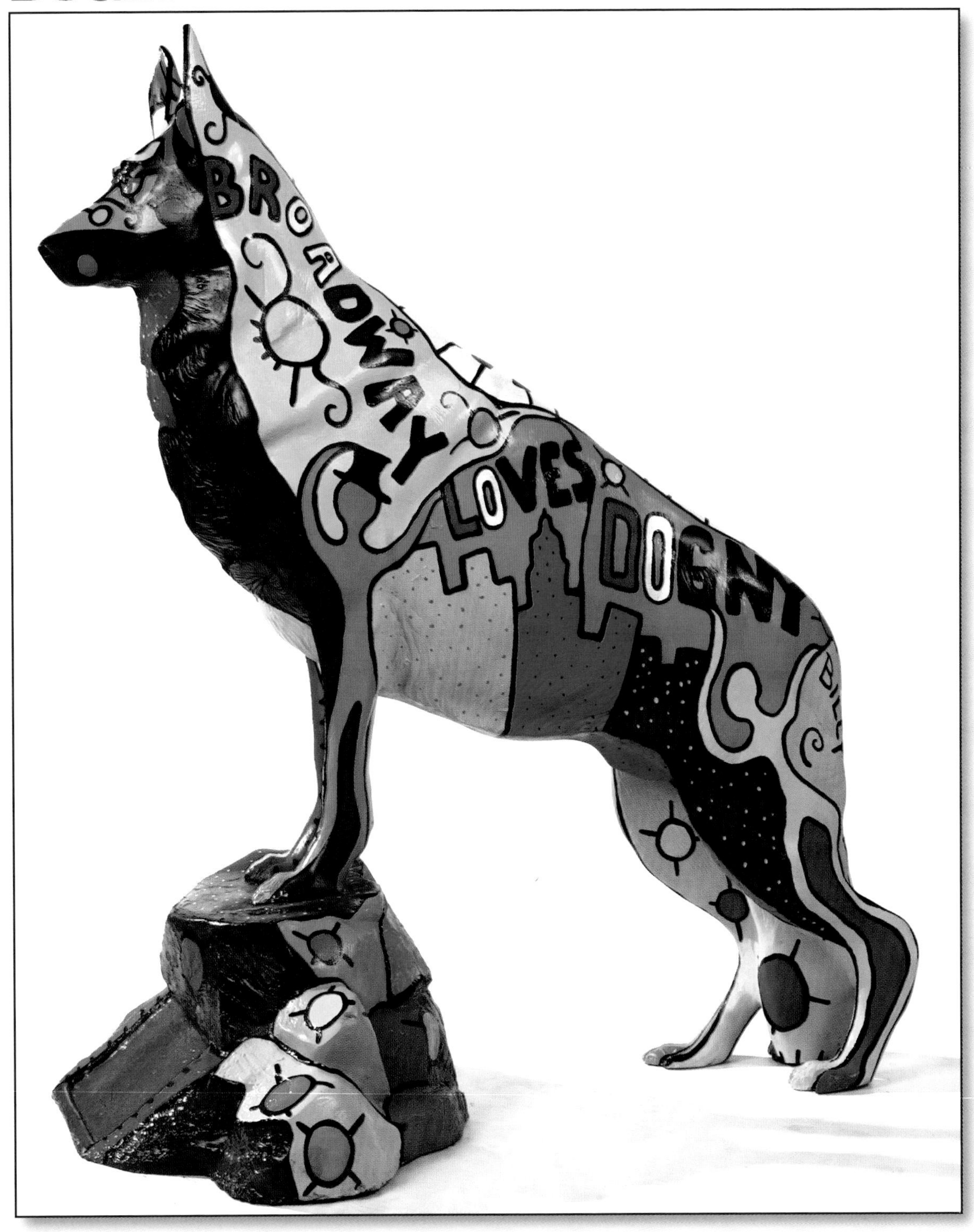

Broadway Loves DOGNY

Billy

About the Artwork:

Like its sister sculpture "Show Stoppers," this design conveys the vibrant spirit of Broadway and New York City itself. Standing proudly in Shubert Alley, this sculpture proclaims the love and support the Broadway community extended to *DOGNY — America's Tribute to Search and Rescue Dogs*.

About the Artist:

"Create Your Own Reality" is the mantra that Billy lives by. This self-taught East Village artist was recently featured in a half-page article in the *New York Times* profiling his life. Billy has exhibited his work in New York, Chicago, Cleveland, and Austin, Texas. His list of corporate clients includes the Manhattan Jewish Community Center, Epic Records, Columbia Pictures, Spike Lee/Pizza Hut, and Sara Lee/Chock Full O' Nuts. Billy's mural projects have taken him all over the globe in the form of installations for such notable clients as DOGNY; Cow Parade New York and Las Vegas; Woodstock 99, where Billy designed and painted 2500 feet of murals for the "Peace Wall" surrounding the concert; the backdrop for the "Emerging Artists" stage; and the Broadway and London productions of *Rent*.

 Sponsor: Mr. & Mrs. Ronald H. Menaker

Shower of Affection

Suzanne Couture

About the Artwork:

"Ron Arnold created the concept behind 'Shower of Affection.' The idea of a shower of affection is to symbolize the outpouring of gratitude so many of us felt toward the participants involved in the 9/11 rescue efforts—both canine and human."

About the Artist:

Suzanne Couture is a model maker who has produced models for every conceivable medium. Her reputation has been built on craftsmanship and the ability to turn any idea into a three-dimensional reality.

Sponsor: Saatchi and Saatchi •

The Heart to Save Mankind

Donna Parker

About the Artwork:

"As a lover of the breed, I wanted to convey the huge heart these dogs have for their masters. This is a once-in-a-lifetime chance to give them and the people involved with them the support, appreciation, and recognition they deserve."

About the Artist:

Dogs have always been very special illustration subjects for Donna Parker, who began her formal training at 14 at the Young Artist's studios at the Art Institute of Chicago. She went on to complete her formal education at The Chicago Institute of Fine Arts, Northern Illinois University, and Center for Creative Studies in Detroit, where she studied commercial illustration. Ms. Parker has mastered many media, from mural painting and designing and sewing her own line of teddy bears to designing greeting cards. She lives with her husband, four cats, two birds and one German Shepherd dog named Shewana's Teddy Bear Roosevelt. As a member of the German Shepherd Dog Club of America, she was extremely honored to be chosen by the Club's Board of Directors to be the artist for this statue.

First to the Rescue

Jacqueline Fogel

About the Artwork:

"This sculpture is extremely important to me, because it is a tribute to all of the search and rescue dog owners and handlers who donated their services to helping others after September 11, 2001. Signatures from almost 150 of these selfless volunteers are incorporated onto the body of sculpture. By creating this piece for DOGNY, I hope to give a little back to those who gave so much to us."

About the Artist:

"I am an artist who loves New York and paints watercolors of the city in vibrant color. I also pick up parts of furniture from the streets: porch posts, chair rungs, nuts, bolts, you name it, and with this found material, I create figures that I paint brightly."

 Sponsor: Animal Medical Center and The Iams Company

Robert L. Braun

About the Artwork:

"This sculpture represents the flag and America, having been hit by terrorism, as it absorbs the shock waves. As a nation, we still stand defiant and resolved in our purpose."

About the Artist:

World-renowned artist Robert Braun brings a mix of his personal commitment and passion for wildlife to his masterfully sculpted works of art. He studied art history and sculpting at the University of Di Breira in Milan, Italy. He then received his Masters degree at The London International Film School, where he studied live action and animation. Over the past 20 years, Mr. Braun has created animation, FX's, and artwork for books, museums, and the film industry. Mr. Braun's sculptures are in numerous private collections, as well as The Museum of Scotland, The British Museum of Natural History, and the National Museum of Science, Taiwan.

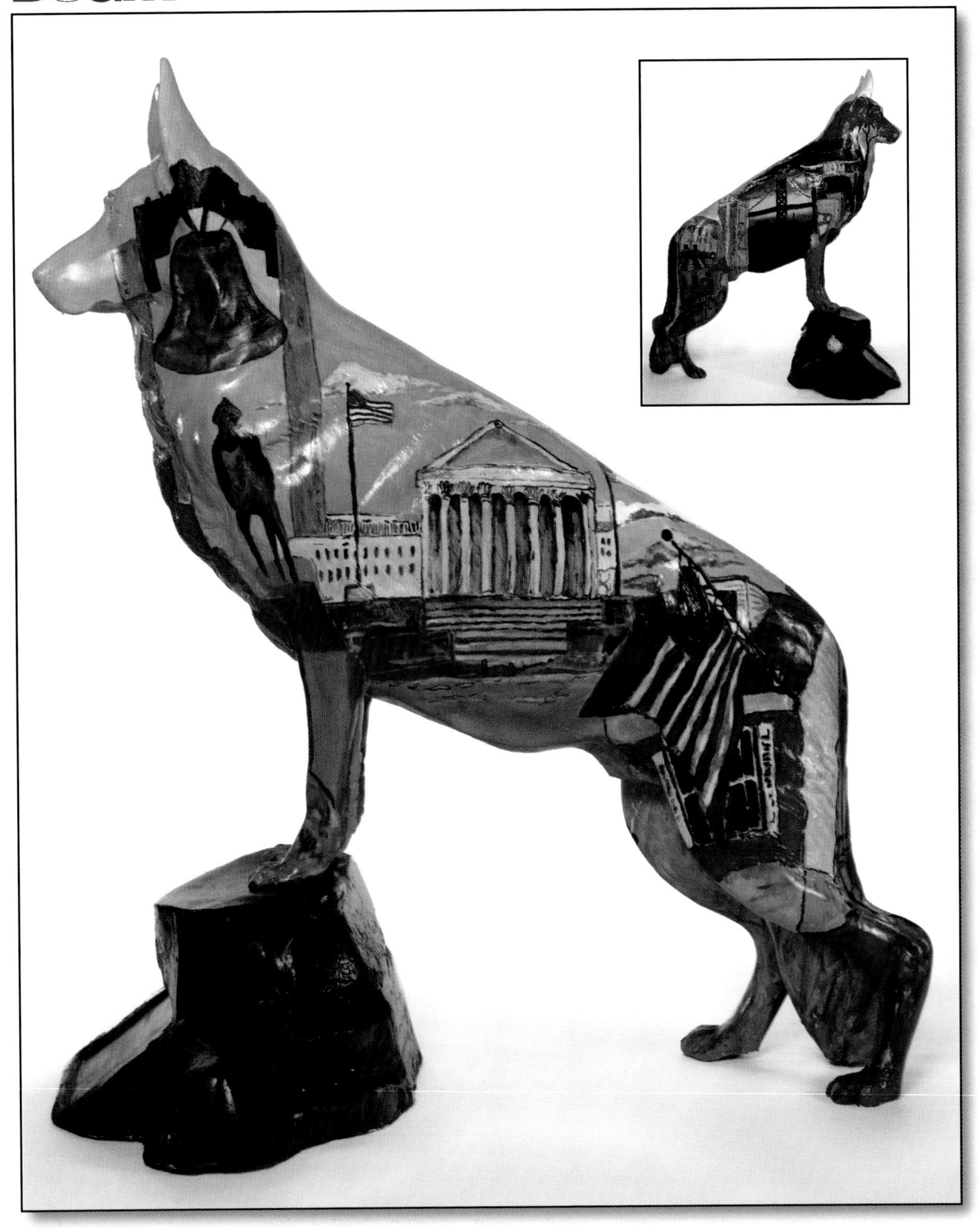

Philly Dog

Mary Ann Paredes

About the Artwork:

"Philly Dog is a visual collection of scenes from the birthplace of our flag, Philadelphia, Pennsylvania. It includes the Betsy Ross House, the Liberty Bell, and the Philadelphia Museum of Fine Arts. Other bits of Philly architecture are included as well, such as the Historic Furness Building, the Old State Building, and the opening of Philadelphia Chinatown. Done in a display of vibrant color, it portrays a beautiful city in a light, spirited, and enjoyable way."

About the Artist:

"I would be lying if I said something profound about my art. I like to paint things that I am familiar with. I suppose that you could say I paint relationships I have with people, things, and events in my life that I believe should only be interesting (truthfully) to me. My style is pretty straightforward. I paint so you know what it is, I like playing with color and texture, and I like to concern myself with composition and design. I think everyone lies almost all the time, and since I'm part of everyone, I try to not lie in one aspect of my life. This is the part I share with an audience, and the irony of it is that to tell the truth I had to be completely quiet."

Dog with Butterflies

Heidi Klum

About the Artwork:

"I participated in DOGNY because I wanted to help out a great cause. I always love opportunities to bring a little life and art to the city. And especially since I've gotten my Jack Russell, Shila, I am a total dog person!"

About the Artist:

Heidi Klum is a star of the fashion world. Having made her breakthrough as the 1998 cover girl for the highly competitive *Sports Illustrated* swimsuit issue and calendar, she has established herself as a top model. Heidi's career is also taking new directions, including television, swimsuit design, jewelry design, and publishing. Her charity involvements include work on behalf of such organizations as the Elizabeth Glazer Pediatric AIDS Foundation. Her paintings have appeared in national magazines.

Sponsor: Staff of The American Kennel Club

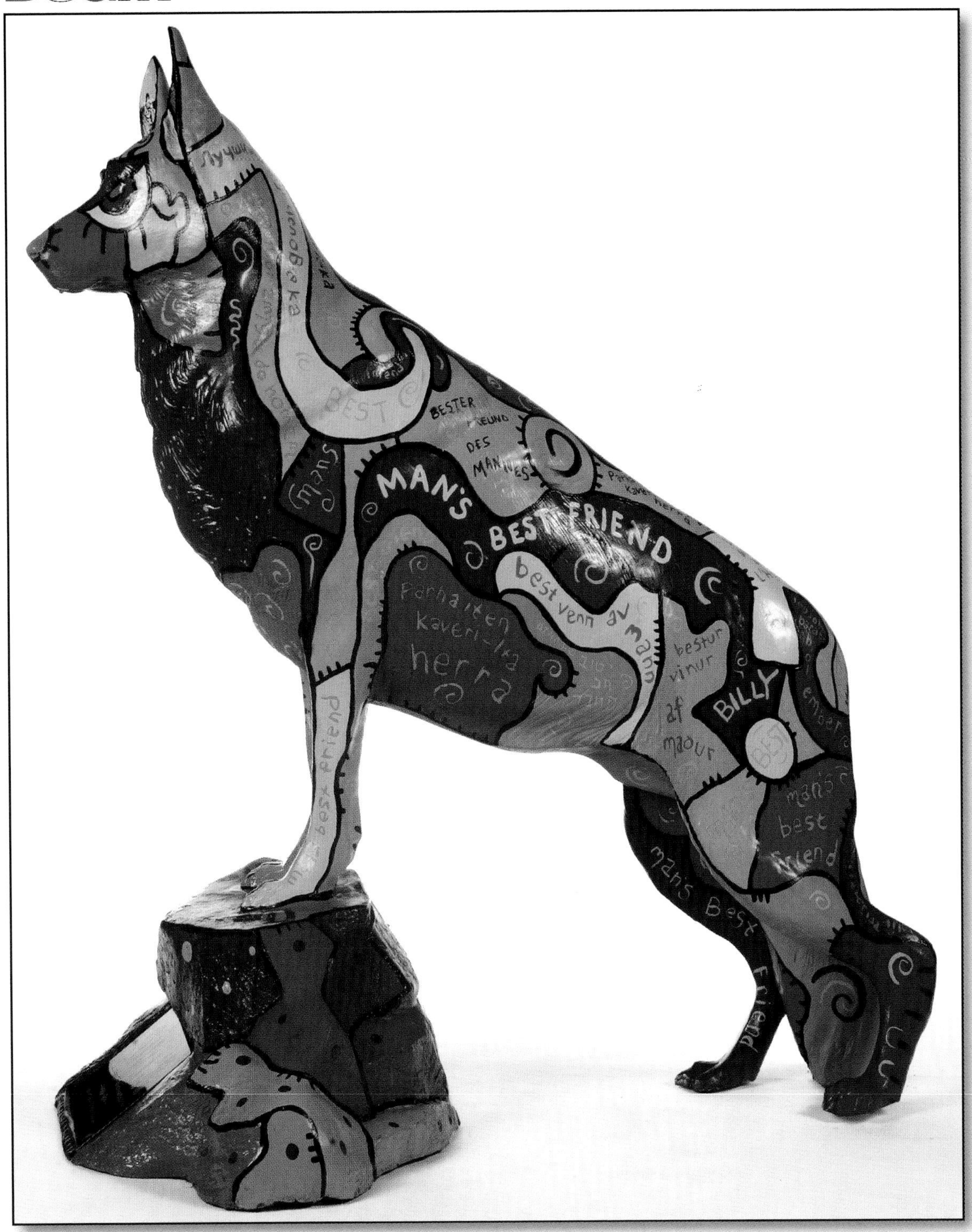

Man's Best Friend

Billy

About the Artwork:

"The idea of 'man's best friend' is universal. To demonstrate this, I've written 'man's best friend' in 27 different languages over a whirling, colorful abstract design."

About the Artist:

"Create Your Own Reality" is the mantra that Billy lives by. This self-taught East Village artist was recently featured in a half-page article in the *New York Times* profiling his life. Billy has exhibited his work in New York, Chicago, Cleveland, and Austin, Texas. His list of corporate clients includes the Manhattan Jewish Community Center, Epic Records, Columbia Pictures, Spike Lee/Pizza Hut, and Sara Lee/Chock Full O' Nuts. Billy's mural projects have taken him all over the globe in the form of installations for such notable clients as DOGNY; Cow Parade New York and Las Vegas; Woodstock 99, where Billy designed and painted 2,500 feet of murals for the "Peace Wall" surrounding the concert; the backdrop for the "Emerging Artists" stage; and the Broadway and London productions of *Rent.*

A World at Peace

Mary Fragapane

About the Artwork:

"A stylized peace dove flies over the American flag and attached to her olive branch is a banner that reads, 'Believe that your world will grow brighter.' The earth is depicted as seen from space, with a draped heart superimposed over it. These are simple, universal images: what we strive for; what we fight for; what we negotiate for—a world at peace."

About the Artist:

Mary Fragapane is known for her figurative paintings representing the beauty of the human spirit. She most recently showed her work at the Epiphany Gallery in Soho, and at Kanvas in the heart of Manhattan's art district, Chelsea. She has shown her work on both coasts and has been the only New York artist invited to participate in the Art for Life charity auction in San Francisco for the last three years. As a muralist, Mary has painted several large-scale murals for both private and public spaces and was one of the artists commissioned to paint for the Woodstock '99 commemorative "Peace Wall," for which she designed and painted over 500 feet of murals.

Setting the Pace

Mike Neville

About the Artwork:

"It was an honor to design this DOGNY sculpture for Pace University in their school colors. I enjoyed creating this piece in an abstract style, reflecting the progressive endeavors of Pace, while still paying tribute to search and rescue dogs."

About the Artist:

Mike Neville has been exhibiting his paintings internationally since 1982. Listed in *Art in America*, his works are in private and corporate collections in London, Paris, Madrid, Zurich, Barcelona, and throughout the U.S. A native of Birmingham, Alabama, Neville studied architecture and music composition before moving to New York City in 1969.

Purple Majesty

Mitchell Meisner

About the Artwork:

This specially painted sculpture changes from shades of purple to green in accordance with changes of the light.

About the Artist:

The Meisner Gallery was responsible for creation of the model and castings of the DOGNY sculptures. Continuing the proud tradition of serving the fine art community, the Meisner Gallery includes sculpture and print publishing, worldwide sculpture distribution, and an advanced acrylic-casting facility. Meisner maintains a large gallery and showroom that was featured on the April 1997 cover of *Art World News*. Located in Farmingdale, New York, the Meisner Gallery has been a springboard for many aspiring artists over the past 30 years.

Sponsors: Park Shore Kennel Club, Chain O'Lakes Kennel Club, and Little Fort Kennel Club, Illinois, USA

Pure Courage

Tracy Monahan

About the Artwork:

The inspiration for the artwork was the purebred dogs that participated in the search and rescue efforts on September 11, 2001. Each AKC-recognized breed that worked at Ground Zero is represented by a head study on the sculpture on a field of blue and white stars, reminiscent of the U.S. flag.

About the Artist:

Tracy Monahan holds a Bachelor of Fine Arts degree from the University of Connecticut, and was a recipient of a scholarship to the Educational Center for the Arts in New Haven, Connecticut. In addition to being an artist, she is a breeder and exhibitor of English Springer Spaniels under the Capulet kennel name. She is also Vice President and Show Chair of the 100-year-old Ladies Kennel Association of America.

Wings of Hope

Interbrand Creative Team

About the Artwork:

The concept was designed to be a memorial to the dogs that served our city and our nation following September 11. It will serve as a memorial to the event and the spirit of humanity. From a distance the dog evokes an angelic image of the animal, but, upon closer inspection, the concept is meant to stimulate thoughts about the events of September 11 and how they changed us as a nation. White represents the selfless and courageous nature of these incredible animals, as well as the pure and optimistic attitude that we need to move forward in our daily lives. The handprints on the dog's shoulder are representative of the relationship that these dogs have with their handlers. They also convey the healing touch of hope.

About the Artist:

The Interbrand New York design team conceived and designed the "Wings of Hope" dog and acknowledges its valued partnership with The Iams Company.

Sponsor: Interbrand Corporation •

Super Star

Wendy Miller's Kids at Art

About the Artwork:

The five 11-year-old children who painted this sculpture all live in New York City and attend after-school art classes at Kids at Art. After drawing different sketches, they all voted and picked one, although they each painted a particular section and used their own style. They were all very moved by 9/11 and very motivated to contribute to the DOGNY project.

About the Artists:

Wendy Miller's Kids at Art provides nurturing, non-competitive art programs for children in New York City. Her studio offers classes and projects for children aged two to 11 that focus on the basics of visual arts. Wendy works with small groups of children so that each young artist's imagination and creativity can be fully stimulated.

Pride

Dean Johnson

About the Artwork:

This sculpture is a symbol of America and shows our confidence in the Red, White, and Blue. The crisp lines and vibrant colors of this sculpture convey our nation's strength, resilience, and dignity.

About the Artist

Dean Johnson is a third-generation artist who started painting at the age of seven at his father's side. Of his art and life, he notes, "Mozart and everyday life are my inspirations. I immerse myself daily in painting and sculpting, so that my life and work become one. Subtle and extraordinary colors are combined with various media creating a three-dimensional, unique, and individual work of art."

Sponsor: The American Kennel Club

Tribute to FEMA K-9 Elvis

Nancy Carey

About the Artwork:

"My specific assignment was to do a portrait of Elvis, the black Labrador rescue dog. I did a side view of the dog, with his FEMA (Federal Emergency Management Agency) vest on, against a backdrop of the American flag. The sketch was easy; painting was harder. After applying three coats of gesso to the statue, I transferred the sketch in pencil. Using acrylics, my husband and I gave the dog a gold undercoat, then painted the stars and stripes. On top of that we painted the black dog, including his red, white and blue collar. During the process, which took about five days, I grew quite attached to the German Shepherd statue and to Elvis. I was sad to see the statue go off to the auto body shop to get a protective acrylic coating."

About the Artist:

"I got involved with the DOGNY project through my husband, Russell Bianca, who works at The American Kennel Club. I was excited about participating: Like most people, I was impressed with the intelligence and skill of these heroic rescue dogs. As an artist, the project sounded interesting and challenging to me. My usual medium is watercolor on paper. I'm thrilled to have taken part in this project, and I'm really looking forward to meeting Elvis in person."

Patriot: American SAR Dog

Dean Johnson

About the Artwork:

A search and rescue dog enshrouded in the American flag represents all of the canines, regardless of breed, who work with their handlers to save citizens of our communities every day. SAR dogs are even our ambassadors when they work abroad to help save disaster victims in other nations. SAR dogs know no boundaries.

About the Artist

Dean Johnson is a third-generation artist who started painting at the age of seven at his father's side. Of his art and life, he notes: "Mozart and everyday life are my inspirations. I immerse myself daily in painting and sculpting, so that my life and work become one. Subtle and extraordinary colors are combined with various media creating a three-dimensional, unique and individual work of art."

Sponsor: Triple Crown Dog Academy

Above and Beyond

AMERICAN KENNEL CLUB · AKC · INCORPORATED ®

Donna Nasr

About the Artwork:

The design on this sculpture incorporates the blue sky and clouds of the heavens and the soft wings and halo of an angel. It suggests the rescue dog as a peaceful, innocent, and otherworldly creature.

About the Artist:

"I am a New York City–based freelance illustrator. I also do pet portraiture and I love animals. I attended Music & Art High School, Parsons School of Design, and SUNY New Paltz. To me, dogs are loyal and unconditionally loving creatures, and divine by nature. People who don't get to experience this kind of companionship in their lives truly miss out."

Freedom Dog

Billy

About the Artwork:

"Freedom: It's what America is based on, it's who we are. I've illustrated this by using the symbols of the American flag, a peace sign over the eye, and the word 'Freedom' boldly written over the back of the dog. A simple concept; a powerful word—freedom."

About the Artist:

"Create Your Own Reality" is the mantra that Billy lives by. This self-taught East Village artist was recently featured in a half-page article in the *New York Times* profiling his life. Billy has exhibited his work in New York, Chicago, Cleveland, and Austin, Texas. His list of corporate clients includes the Manhattan Jewish Community Center, Epic Records, Columbia Pictures, Spike Lee/Pizza Hut, and Sara Lee/Chock Full O' Nuts. Billy's mural projects have taken him all over the globe in the form of installations for such notable clients as DOGNY; Cow Parade New York and Las Vegas; Woodstock 99, where Billy designed and painted 2500 feet of murals for the "Peace Wall" surrounding the concert, and the backdrop for the "Emerging Artists" stage; and the Broadway and London productions of *Rent.*

DOGNY

Paws for Peace

Michael McCartney

About the Artwork:

"Paws for Peace" features many purebred dogs showing their own patriotic spirit. German Shepherds, Pembroke Welsh Corgis, Bloodhounds... no matter what breed, our canine companions are loyal citizens, too!

About the Artist:

For the past 25 years, Mike McCartney has been a commercial artist living in Door County, Wisconsin. He started his career by setting up his easel and drawing caricatures of people at local art shows, then worked his way into the commercial art world specializing in whimsical art. The McCartney family attended their first dog show, a Great Dane national specialty, on Labor Day weekend in 1991. McCartney started doing caricatures ringside, and word spread quickly about his style of capturing a dog's personality in any situation. His collection of designs features 150 different breeds, and he promises to keep them interesting by continuously adding new artwork from all the input received from animal lovers across the country.

Santo

Anne Hall

About the Artwork:

This sculpture was inspired by Ms. Hall's dog, Paquita, by tattoo art in countries ranging from India to America, and by a long tradition of religious iconographic sculptures. The inscription on Santo reads "Dedicated to the Memory of Dogs Who Gave Their Lives to Strangers."

About the Artist:

Anne Hall is both a painter and photographer living in New York City. She graduated with a BA in Fine Art from Oberlin College. Her work has been shown at the Smithsonian Institution, The Kennedy Center for Performing Art, Firelands Association of Visual Art, as well as on Animal Planet.

Miró Dog

Yuichi Tanabe

About the Artwork:

"Miró Dog is inspired by the work of Joan Miró. The world of Miró is conveyed through the colors, shapes, patterns, and forms of the design. The sculpture brings Miró's brilliant creativity to life in the substantial form of the dog."

About the Artist:

Yuichi Tanabe was born in Japan in 1956 and is a permanent resident in the U.S. He graduated from Osaka Art University in Japan and has worked as an industrial designer for Panasonic in Japan and as a graphic designer for several organizations in the New York area. He has exhibited his fine art works in Osaka, Tokyo, and Toyama in Japan; in Bridgeport, Connecticut; and Barrytown, New York. Yuichi's motivation as an artist is to connect the worlds of science and spirituality through his art.

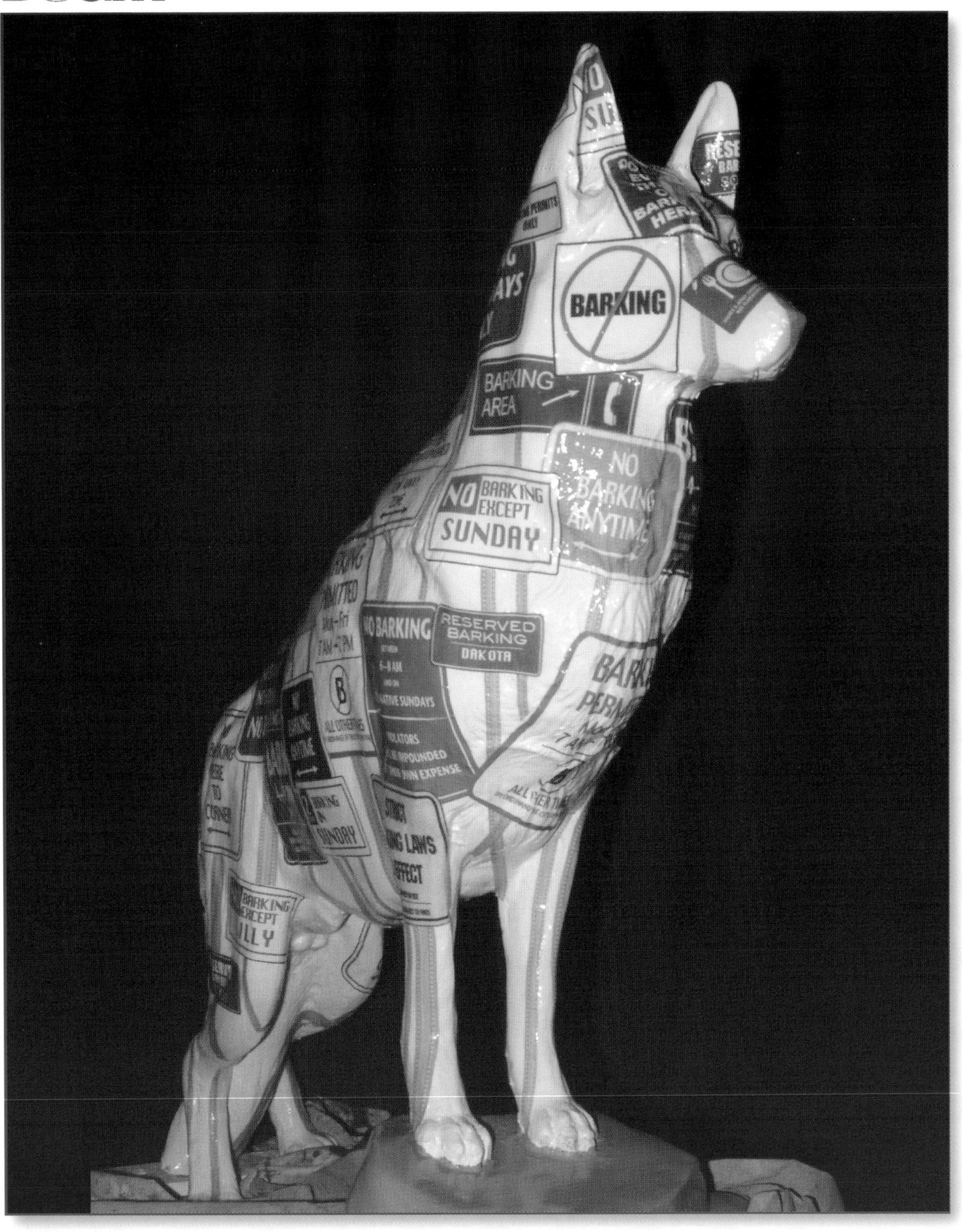

Barking Rules and Regulations

Ellen Hanauer

About the Artwork:

"If you are a dog and are planning on coming to New York, you'd better heed the city street signs, because strict barking laws are in effect here. 'No barking between 6-8 a.m. and on alternative Sundays' and 'Bark here all day for just $6.50' are but a few of the plethora of signs that dot the city. Seems easy enough to follow, until you read the fine print: 'Bark by 6:30 a.m. and chase your tail each hour on the hour' is an example of the strict regulations you can easily miss. Make no bones about it—New York is a great town to visit, but don't leave your reading glasses at the curb!"

About the Artist:

Ellen Hanauer is a sculptor whose work has been described as "original, visceral, and organic." She has exhibited nationally in museums, galleries, and universities. Hanauer's installation, "A Circle of Women," was selected for exhibition in 2001 New Jersey Arts Annual: Crossing Boundaries at the Noyes Museum of Art, New Jersey.

Breuna Baine Mertens

About the Artwork:

The reports that search and rescue dogs had to retire because of the 9/11 aftermath inspired this sculpture.

About the Artist:

Breuna Baine Mertens is a designer at Landor Associates in Cincinnati, Ohio. Breuna has worked as a graphic designer and professor of design for over 10 years, and holds a BFA from Savannah College of Art and Design and a MFA in Visual Communications from Auburn University. She lives in Southgate, Kentucky, with her husband, son, and dog.

A Tribute to Canine Heroes

Dean Johnson

About the Artwork:

This sculpture draws its inspiration from the American flag. Elegant and complex, it conveys the spirit and patriotism behind every search and rescue operation.

About the Artist

Dean Johnson is a third-generation artist who started painting at the age of seven at his father's side. Of his art and life, Dean Johnson notes: "Mozart and everyday life are my inspirations. I immerse myself daily in painting and sculpting, so that my life and work become one. Subtle and extraordinary colors are combined with various media, creating a three-dimensional, unique and individual work of art."

Night Sky Dog

Marina Tsesarskaya

About the Artwork:

This sculpture shows the constellations of the universe and suggests a strong connection between the heavenly and the heroic search and rescue dog.

About the Artist:

The work of Marina Tesarskaya has been presented in solo and group exhibitions in New York City, Poland, Ukraine, Russia, and Canada. Her work has been commissioned for several books, including original etchings for *Seven Strings*, a work about the 19th-century poet, Lesya, and original work for children's books published in Kiev.

Military Dog

Michael Cuomo

About the Artwork:

"In the changing times that confront us all, I was inspired to create this sense of exchange of what is animal and human. My work reaches out to the heroism that serves our country to make the world a better place to live."

About the Artist:

"Prior to 9/11, I was never consciously patriotic, but being in New York City and living in the shocking reality of that day, I arose to a different plateau of awareness. Previously unimportant symbols became important to me—the flag, our country, and my city. These new works include past methods of expression and new unknown values. My earlier projects were more sculptural in nature, including construction and woodworking, and it seemed natural to bring these techniques into my new works."

Sergeant

Nicholas Vito Macchio

About the Artwork:

"I named this dog 'Sergeant' in honor of the brave men and women who lead not by appointment, but by honor, duty, and service to fellow man. Like the sergeant in the trenches with his charges, this leadership comes from within. The strong sergeant stands a silent vigil close to the ground, close to his people, ever ready to give his all—even if that means his life."

About the Artist:

Born into an artistic Italian/Greek family in the Hell's Kitchen district of New York City, Nicholas V. Macchio was already exhibiting and winning awards for his art by the age of five. After graduating with a degree in advertising art and design, Nicholas accepted a position as Assistant Art Director for a major magazine and then went on to freelance work. He became involved in the animal rights movement, and for over nine years volunteered his services and artistic capabilities to this cause, creating and donating all artwork (posters, paintings, newsletters, banners, etc.).

Sponsors: Onofrio Dog Shows, LLC, Oklahoma City Kennel Club, Inc., Canadian Valley Kennel Club, Town and Country Kennel Club, and Mid-Del Tinker Kennel Club

Angel

Vera Wang

About the Artwork:

"Angel" is Vera Wang's personal tribute to canine search and rescue. Simple, elegant, and understated, this sequin-covered sculpture pays tribute to the quiet countenance of the modern working dog.

About the Artist:

There's a reason why the most stylish women in the world turn to Vera Wang when it comes to their big moment: a Vera Wang design ensures that she will be modern and sensual—whether she's walking up the red carpet or down the wedding aisle. In just over ten years, the Vera Wang label has come to represent all that is sleek and sophisticated, from Vera's internationally acclaimed wedding dresses to her ultra-chic evening wear. Vera has created an aspirational world that speaks to urbane women who seek understated elegance and spare lines. From its 1990 inception, the company has thrived, with collections that extend to ready-to-wear, fur, and footwear.

Union Pride

Nicholas Vito Macchio

About the Artwork:

"As a former teamster, I understand and appreciate what a strong union can do for the American worker. This sculpture symbolizes all that is good, honest, and just in the union cause. No matter the union or worker, the goal and the dreams are shared. The American worker is the lifeblood of the economy, and the union is the shield and protector of these workers."

About the Artist:

Born into an artistic Italian/Greek family in the Hell's Kitchen district of New York City, Nicholas V. Macchio was already exhibiting and winning awards for his art by the age of five. After graduating with a degree in advertising art and design, Nicholas accepted a position as Assistant Art Director for a major magazine and then went on to freelance work. He became involved in the animal rights movement, and for over nine years volunteered his services and artistic capabilities to this cause, creating and donating all artwork (posters, paintings, newsletters, banners, etc.).

Sponsor: CSEA/AFSCME

Miró Dog II

Yuichi Tanabe

About the Artwork:

"Miró Dog is inspired by the work of Joan Miró. The world of Miró is conveyed through the colors, shapes, patterns, and forms of the design. The sculpture brings Miró's brilliant creativity to life in the substantial form of the dog."

About the Artist:

Yuichi Tanabe was born in Japan in 1956 and is a permanent resident of the U.S. He graduated from Osaka Art University in Japan and has worked as an industrial designer for Panasonic in Japan and as a graphic designer for several organizations in the New York area. He has exhibited his fine art works in Osaka, Tokyo, and Toyama in Japan; in Bridgeport, Connecticut; and Barrytown, New York. Yuichi's motivation as an artist is to connect the worlds of science and spirituality through his art.

Footprints of Hope

Robert L. Braun

About the Artwork:

"Footprints of Hope" reminds us that many animals can be of assistance to mankind, in a variety of scenarios. Whether canine, feline, bovine, or porcine, animals play an important role in our lives.

About the Artist:

World-renowned artist Robert Braun brings a mix of his personal commitment and passion for wildlife to his masterfully sculpted works of art. He studied art history and sculpting at the University of Di Breira in Milan, Italy. He then received his Masters degree at The London International Film School, where he studied live action and animation. Over the past 20 years, Mr. Braun has created animation, FX's, and artwork for books, museums, and the film industry. Mr. Braun's sculptures are in numerous private collections, as well as The Museum of Scotland, The British Museum of Natural History, and the National Museum of Science, Taiwan.

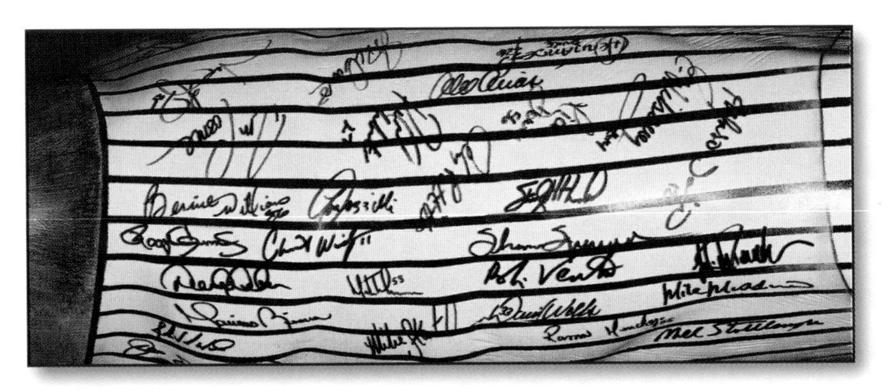

126 • *Sponsor: Eukanuba Dog Foods/The Iams Company*

America's Pastime

Robert L. Braun

About the Artwork:

Painted in "Bronx Bomber" pinstripes, this DOGNY sculpture was signed by members of the New York Yankees. Among the autographs are signatures from Joe Torre, Roger Clemens, Orlando Hernandez, Sterling Hitchcock, Steve Karsay, Ramiro Mendoza, Mike Mussina, Andy Pettitte, Mariano Rivera, Mike Stanton, Jeff Weaver, David Wells, Jorge Posada, Chris Widger, Alex Arias, Ron Coomer, Jason Giambi, Derek Jeter, Alfonso Soriano, Robin Ventura, Enrique Wilson, Shane Spencer, John Vander Wal, Rondell White, Bernie Williams, Mel Stottlemyre, Lee Mazzilli, Mike Thurman, and Rick Downing.

About the Artist:

World-renowned artist Robert Braun brings a mix of his personal commitment and passion for wildlife to his masterfully sculpted works of art. He studied art history and sculpting at the University of Di Breira in Milan, Italy. He then received his Masters degree at The London International Film School, where he studied live action and animation. Over the past 20 years, Mr. Braun has created animation, FX's, and artwork for books, museums, and the film industry. Mr. Braun's sculptures are in numerous private collections, as well as The Museum of Scotland, The British Museum of Natural History, and the National Museum of Science, Taiwan.

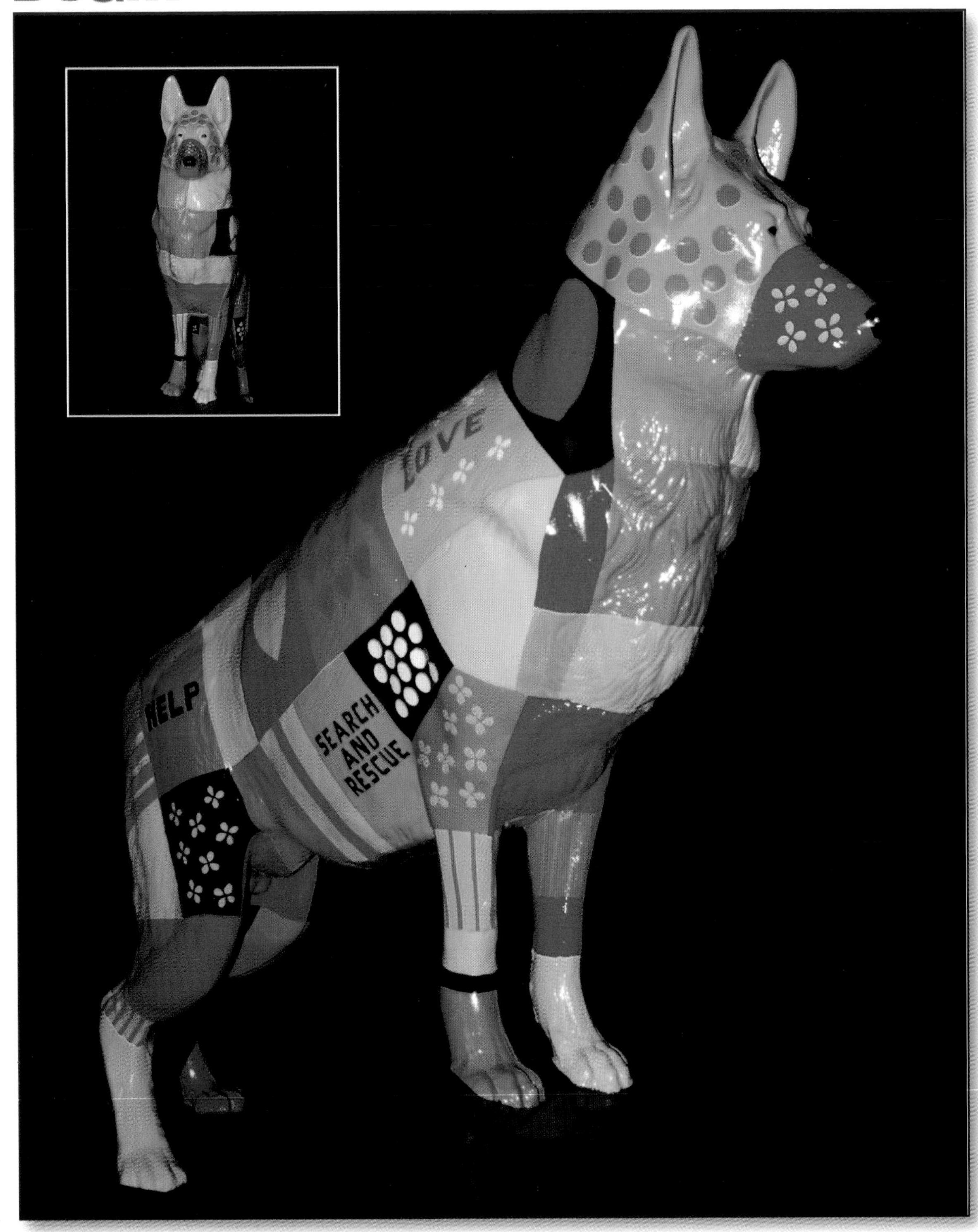

Patchwork Dog

Jacqueline Fogel

About the Artwork:

"I chose to do a patchwork dog to show the love and devotion these brave search and rescue canines bring to their jobs."

About the Artist:

"I am an artist who loves New York and paints watercolors of the city in vibrant color. I also pick up parts of furniture from the streets: porch posts, chairs, rugs, nuts, bolts, you name it, and with this found material, I create figures that I paint brightly. "

Bravo

Daniel Mulligan

About the Artwork:

"The dog's name is Bravo. Mrs. Wilpon, the sponsor, asked me to paint the dog in a realistic manner. It wears a protective bib, which is painted in the baseball colors of the New York Mets (blue and orange). This reflects the pride that the Mets team has for this cause."

About the Artist:

Mr. Mulligan is a 41-year-old self-taught artist, native to New Jersey. From the age of 16, he has had a strong interest in landscapes, animals, locomotives, and still life, which he paints in an academic or photo-realistic manner. He has exhibited at galleries in New York City and California and has been featured in many publications.

Sponsor: The New York Mets Foundation and Mr. and Mrs. Fred Wilpon

Appendix I: About the American Kennel Club (AKC)

The American Kennel Club was founded on September 17, 1884, as an independent, nonprofit organization devoted to the advancement and welfare of purebred dogs.

The AKC's membership is comprised of approximately 560 autonomous dog clubs whose Delegates elect the AKC's Board of Directors and vote on rule changes.

The AKC is the principal registry agency for purebred dogs in the United States, registering in excess of one million dogs a year. Records for the more than 40 million dogs registered since 1878 are stored at the AKC.

The objectives of the AKC are to adopt and enforce uniform rules regulating and governing dog shows and field trials; to regulate the conduct of persons interested in exhibiting, running, breeding, registering, purchasing, and selling dogs; to detect, prevent, and punish fraud in connection therewith; to protect the interest of its members; to maintain and publish an official stud book and an official kennel gazette; and generally to do everything to advance the study, breeding, exhibiting, running, and maintenance of the purity of thoroughbred dogs.

The AKC houses a library of more than 17,000 volumes of canine-related material. The library is open to the public. The AKC also exhibits and stores an extensive collection of paintings, statuary, and canine memorabilia.

The *AKC Gazette* is the official magazine of the AKC. The AKC also publishes *American Kennel Club puppies* magazine, *AKC Dog Care and Training*, *The Complete Dog Book* and *The Complete Dog Book for Kids*.

The AKC also offers videos for each of the AKC-recognized breeds, as well as videos on care and training, such as the "Breed ID Series" and "The Right Dog for You."

The American Kennel Club Canine Health Foundation funds original research in canine health, with a specific focus on canine genetics. The AKC also funds research projects at some of the nation's most prominent veterinary institutions and awards veterinary scholarships to students pursuing canine studies.

The Companion Animal Recovery (CAR) program provides a nationwide pet identification and recovery service. All companion animals identified by microchip and/or tattoo are eligible for enrollment in the database. Service is provided 24 hours, 365 days a year. The phone number is 1-800-252-7894, email: found@akc.org (these are for CAR only).

The American Kennel Club Museum of the Dog, located in St. Louis, Missouri, is home to the world's finest collection of art devoted to the dog. The 14,000 square foot facility displays over 500 original paintings, drawings, watercolors, prints, sculptures in bronze and porcelain, and a variety of decorative arts objects depicting man's best friend throughout the age.

Following the events of September 11, 2001, the American Kennel Club Companion Animal Recovery (CAR) Corporation Canine Support and Relief Fund was established to aid the canine search and rescue units that participated in the recovery efforts at the World Trade Center, the Pentagon and Pennsylvania, and the veterinary organizations that supported them.

Visit the AKC online at www.akc.org.

Appendix II: About Search and Rescue (SAR) Dogs

The bond between humans and canines is an ancient one. Dogs and people have lived together for millennia. Over the course of our history together, dogs and humans have worked as teams to find food, work with livestock, and serve our country. Search and Rescue is arguably the dog's most noble vocation. Dogs have acted on behalf of lost or injured humans as early as 1750. The Canine Search and Rescue teams of today put the canine-human bond into practice by tracking and finding victims of crime, avalanches, earthquakes, floods—and as we all witnessed on September 11, 2001—terrorism.

An estimated 300 Search and Rescue Dogs and their handlers offered their services to the recovery efforts at the World Trade Center. The events of September 11 prompted the largest response of United States Urban Search and Rescue in the history of the FEMA network. Twenty-four of the 28 FEMA Urban Search and Rescue teams were deployed, with 20 teams working at the World Trade Center and four in Washington. The FEMA teams, consisting of four dogs per team, represented 19 states. The New York City Police K9 Unit deployed all of its German Shepherd Dogs for the grueling task of finding victims in the rubble. In addition to official, government-sponsored teams, several volunteer Search and Rescue Dog teams arrived from all over the world to help with the Search and Recovery efforts.

Search and Rescue dogs represent a variety of breeds, the most common of which are German Shepherd Dogs, Labrador Retrievers, and Golden Retrievers.

Working with their handlers, Search and Rescue Dogs find lost children, Alzheimer's patients who have wandered from their homes, victims of drownings, avalanches, floods, tornadoes and other disasters. And incredibly, many of them do it not as professionals, but as volunteers.

Their dedication is even more incredible when you realize how much training is involved. Preparing a team for its first mission takes twice-a-week practices for a solid year. Handlers must learn land navigation, map and compass, wilderness survival, and other skills. They practice rigorously throughout their lives to keep those skills sharp.

In a time when disaster preparedness is so crucial, DOGNY seeks to ensure that we will never be short of resources for our nation's Search and Rescue organizations. In the words of The NYPD K-9 Unit's Lt. Dan Donadio, "What we do is needed now more than ever."

Appendix III: *Where the Sculptures Were Exhibited*

In the late summer and fall of 2002, the DOGNY sculptures were on display in the streets of New York's five boroughs, as well as at the Orlando Museum of Art. Sculptures with an * in front of them are on permanent display at their locations.

*9/11 . . . . .96, 97
Animal Medical Center, 510 East 62nd Street, New York, New York

Above and Beyond 110
Riverside Park, West 105th Street and Riverside Dr., New York, New York

All Breeds and Bones 33
Engine 16, 234 East 29th Street, New York, New York

America's Pastime 126, 127
The American Kennel Club, 260 Madison Avenue, New York, New York

American Pedigree 86
Police Academy, 235 East 20th Street, New York, New York

Angel 122
The American Kennel Club, 260 Madison Avenue, New York, New York

Aurora: Angel of Rescue 66
101 Park Avenue at East 41st Street, New York, New York

Bahama Dog 87
Teddy Roosevelt Park, West 81st Street and Columbus Avenue, New York, New York

Barking Rules & Regulations . .116
530 11th Street, Brooklyn, New York

Bone-A-Fide Hero 44
Washington Square Park, West 4th Street and LaGuardia Place, New York, New York

*Bone-A-Fide Patriot 90
Lehman Brothers Park, 745 Seventh Avenue at 49th Street, New York, New York

Brave New World 53
Engine 21, 238 East 40th Street, New York, New York

Bravo 129
575 Fifth Avenue, New York, New York

Broadway Loves DOGNY 92
Shubert Alley, Broadway between West 44th and 45th Streets, New York, New York

Caught in the Search 52
5 Penn Plaza, 33rd Street and 8th Avenue, New York, New York

Celebrate Our NYC Heroes 32
Engine 76, 145 West 100th Street, New York, New York

Comic Strip Canine 84
888 7th Avenue, New York, New York

Courage 60, 61
Engine 4, 42 South Street, New York, New York

Day and Night 43
Chelsea Waterside Park, West 22nd Street and 11th Avenue, New York, New York

Dog Love Power 76
9 Metrotech Center, Brooklyn, New York

Dog with Butterflies 99
GM Building, 767 Fifth Avenue at East 58th Street, New York, New York

Doggy Dog 58
Engine 35, 2282 3rd Avenue, New York, New York

Dogwood 71
Mount Sinai Hospital, 1190 Fifth Avenue, New York, New York

The Eyes of Hope, the Heart of a Hero 70
Engine 58, 1367 Fifth Avenue, New York, New York

Faces of the World 63
Engine 162, 256 Nelson Avenue, Staten Island, New York

First to the Rescue 95
Engine 152, 256 Hylan Boulevard, Staten Island, New York

Flags of the World 13
Carl Schurz Park, East 86th and East River Drive, New York, New York

Footprints of Hope 125
1466 Broadway, New York, New York

Freedom Begins with Me 42
32nd Precinct, 250 West 135th Street, New York, New York

Freedom Dog 111
Engine 43, 1901 Sedgwick Avenue, Bronx, New York

Galaxy Dog 56
1 Police Plaza, New York, New York

A Girl and Her Dog 34
Carl Schurz Park, East 86th and East River Drive, New York, New York

Heart of Gold 35
Engine 55, 363 Broome Street, New York, New York

The Heart to Save Mankind . . .94
East River Esplanade, East River at East 60th Street Pavillion, New York, New York

I Love NY Search and Rescue . .48
6th Precinct, 233 West 10th Street, New York, New York

In Dog We Trust 82
Food Emporium, 316 Greenwich Street, New York, New York

Iris's Irises 49
Tavern on the Green, Central Park at West 67th Street, New York, New York

K-9 Ladder 83
The American Kennel Club, 260 Madison Avenue, New York, New York

K-9 Police 40
The American Kennel Club, 260 Madison Avenue, New York, New York

Landog 117
Police Academy, 235 East 20th Street, New York, New York

Let Freedom Ring 78
Empire State Building, 350 Fifth Avenue between West 33rd and 34th Streets, New York, New York

Liberty .67
Gateway Plaza, Battery Park City, New York, New York

Liberty's Light 55
Engine 207, 172 Tillary Street, Brooklyn, New York

Majesty .65
Engine 154, 3730 Victory Boulevard, Staten Island, New York

Major 18, 19
Toys 'R Us, Times Square, New York, New York

Man's Best Friend 100
Madison Square Park, Madison Avenue between East 23rd and East 26th Streets, New York, New York

Index of Sponsors and Contributors

(Corporations, Clubs, and Individuals)

Corporate Sponsors:

The Iams Company
The Hartz Mountain Company
FedEx
JPMorgan Chase
The American Kennel Club
American Kennel Club Companion
Animal Recovery
A&P
Ahold USA
Animal Medical Center
Animal Planet
Bank One
Bayer
Bollinger, Inc.
Canine Chronicle
CSEA/AFSCME
The Chubb Group of Insurance Companies
Dog News
Ernst & Young Foundation
Gibson Dunn & Crutcher LLP
Hill's Pet Nutrition
Insignia/ESG
Interbrand Corporation
King Features Syndicate
Landor Associates
Lefrak Organization
Lehman Brothers
Loews Hotels
Major League Baseball
Merial
Nestlé Purina Petcare Company
New York Mets Foundation Mr. and Mrs. Fred Wilpon
News Corporation/New York Post
NJ Pets
Novartis Animal Health US, Inc.
Nutro Products, Inc.
Onofrio Dog Shows LLC
Pace University
Pedigree/Master Foods USA
Petland Discounts
Petco Foundation
Pfizer Animal Health Group
Philip Ross Industries
Polo Ralph Lauren
Reckson Associates
Remington Arms Company
Saatchi & Saatchi
Telford Veterinary Hospital
Triple Crown Dog Academy
Veterinary Pet Insurance
Vietnam Veterans of America, New York State Council

Corporate Contributors:

American Airlines
American Express Foundation
Cine Magnetics, Inc.
Davis Polk & Wardwell
Dog Show Photography: Tom and Cathi Di Giacomo
Dogs in Review
Doll-McGuinness
The DuPont Corporation Automotive Paint Division
FedEx Metro NYC Retail
Interzoo Show
The Kennel Club Charitable Trust
Kraftsman Group, Inc.
Maran's Autobody, Woodside, NY
Marzocco Dun-Rite Autobody Inc.
McConville Photography
Mountain Range Farms, L.P.
Originals by Springer
Pepsi Cola Company
Regency, A Loews Hotel
Republic Mills, Inc.
Security Packaging Company, Inc.
Simkins Industries, Inc.
Specialty Pet Supplies, Inc.
Tiffany & Co. in honor of Karen LeFrak

Club Sponsors & Contributors:

The Alaskan Malamute Club of America
American Sealyham Terrier Club
The Atlanta Kennel Club, Inc.
Bichon Frise Club of Northern New Jersey, Inc.
Bronx County Kennel Club
Chain O'Lakes Kennel Club (Illinois)
Channel City Kennel Club
Dandie Dinmont Terrier Club of America, Inc.
Detroit Kennel Club
Dog Judges Association of America
Evergreen Afghan Hound Club
Farmington Valley Kennel Club on behalf of Double A Veterinary Hospital
Finger Lakes Kennel Club, Inc.
Fort Worth Kennel Club
German Shepherd Dog Club of America
Greater Collin Kennel Club
Great Dane Club of San Diego
Harrisburg Kennel Club
Huntington Kennel Club, Inc.
Jupiter-Tequesta Dog Club
Labrador Retriever Club
Langley Kennel Club
Lincolnland Basset Hound Club
Little Fort Kennel Club
Long Island Coalition of Dog Fanciers
Long Island Kennel Club
Manitowoc County Kennel Club
Marion Ohio Kennel Club
Mid Florida Judges Study Group
The Middle Peninsula Kennel Club
Nashville Kennel Club
Naugatuck Valley Kennel Club
New Brunswick Kennel Club
Oklahoma Sooner Circuit, Inc., consisting of Oklahoma City Kennel Club, Inc., Canadian Valley Kennel Club, Town and Country Kennel Club, and Mid-Del Tinker Kennel Club
Onate Trail Dog Fanciers Association
Park Shore Kennel Club
Penn Ridge Kennel Club, Inc.
Riverhead Kennel Club
Santa Clara Valley Kennel Club
Scottsdale Dog Fanciers Association
Somerset Hills Kennel Club
Springfield Kennel Club
Sussex Spaniel Club of America, Inc.
Texas Kennel Club, Inc.
Trenton Kennel Club, Inc.

Individual Sponsors:

Dr. and Mrs. Sheldon Adler
Ellen M. Charles and Melissa Cantacuzène in memory of Adelaide Close Riggs
D.B.O.
Deramus Foundation
David and Cherilyn Frei
Jeffrey Pepper and the Stella and Arthur Pepper Foundation, Inc.
Walter F. Goodman
Sandra & Howard Hoffen, Monica, Tux, & Michael

Gilbert S. Kahn
Amy Kiell and Harvey Schwartz: Pebbles' Run Samoyeds
Janet Lange
Sam and Marion Lawrence
Howard M. and Thea Lorber
Linda and Mickey Low
Mr. & Mrs. Ronald Menaker
Laura J. Niles Foundation
Corey and Alicia Pinkston
Marilyn Polite
Anne Radice in honor of Prof. Iris Love
Mr. and Mrs. Roger Rechler
Daryl and Steven Roth Foundation
Cecelia Ruggles and J.R.
Mr. and Mrs. Martin Sosnoff
John Spurling
Lillian Vernon Foundation

Individual Contributors:

Svetlana Adler
Rich Ahlers
Karen Aiello and Family, Lisa Sloane and Bob and Sally Nason in memory of Monti
The AKC Call Center Staff
Dolores Alonso
George and Mary Ann Alston
Charles and Sharon Anderson
Maria Andriano
June and Sam Annitto
Anonymous
Michiko Araki
Christina Lang Assael
Howard and Barbara Atlee
Kathleen and Roland Augustine
Mr. and Mrs. Roger N. Ayres
Joseph and Greer Baffuto
Drs. Mary Burch and Jon Bailey
Ellen Barry
Constance M. Barton
Noreen and Carl Baxter
Joanne Mary Beacon
Reggie Beard
Tiffany Beard
Mrs. Charles Bell
Monique Y. Bell
Pamela Bennerson
George Berger
Robert Berne
Marsha and Seth Bernstein in honor of Daphna Straus
Tanya Bielski
William D. Birch
Bobby Birdsong
Nancy M. Bischoff
Melanie Blair
David and Phyllis Blevins
Eileen Bolton
Anne Bolus
Debra Ann Bonneford
Jesse and Galye Bontecou
Janet and Sanford Borinsky
E.G. and C.J. Brennan
Tony Britt
Jo-Ann Brown and "Chance" in honor and memory of Git Ander, canine hero
Carol A. Bryant
Robert and Lorraine Burg
Ms. Linda Lee Burke
David Buttgereit
Denise LeFrak Calicchio in honor of Karen LeFrak
Sherry Campbell
Valarie and Delroy Campbell
Delaine W. Cantrell
Michael Allway and Anne C. Caplan
Wendy N. Carduner
Lisa Cecin
Sue Cerbone
Christine Chadsey
Jessie Chanoine
Alfred & Patricia Cheauré
Dale C. Christensen, Jr. and Patricia Hewitt
Peter A. Cohen
Kristin Colvin
Jacqueline Cook
Sharon Cook
Stephen Costallos
James and Agnes Crowley
Patricia M. Cruz
Tim Cunningham
Dennis and Arline Cutler
Nicholas and Rosalee D'Altilio
William G. and Cathy H. Daugherty
Carrie De Young
Catherine M. Deangelis
Janet Ford and James Dearinger
Kirby and Bonita Dennis
Bernard Depinto
Jenny Dickinson
Barbara M. Dille
Sheila and Anthony DiNardo, DMD
Mary M. Donnelly
Janet Doolittle
Jackie Dothard
Bernice and Donald Drapkin
Linda Duncklee
Lois C. Dustin
R. Dean Eagle
Kim Eberley
Mrs. Henry D. Epstein
James and Sue Etheridge
Marjorie L. Everett
Garadine Fair
Malina and Edward Farshtey
Sharon Faucette
Victoria Field and The AKC Learning and Development Department
Leslie Finch
Clark Fiscella
Lester Fisher
The Flaherty Family Foundation
Charlotte Ford
Valerie Franklin
Keith and Shannon Frazier
Albert A. Fried, Jr.
Gary and Stephanie Frye
Kenny and Rita Fulmer
Frieda Furman
Peter and Terri Gaeta
Jan Gaff
Patricia Gallatin in honor of Ch. Friendship Hill Dr. Watson and Ernesto Lara
Rita Gardner
Patricia A. Gellerman
Mr. and Mrs. Peter Georgescu
S. Terri Giannetti and Ted Swedalla Jr.
Alice Giliberti
Tom Glassford
Judy Gold
Harvey and Susan Goldberg
Suzanne and John Golden
Goldsmith Family Charitable Foundation, Inc.
Jerome R. Goldstein
Yvette Gonzalez
Murray Goodman
Rebecca Gordon
Denise and Thomas C. Gorrian
Dr. and Mrs. Eugene Gottlieb
Tilly Grassa
Susan L. Gray
Emilie Greco
Barbara Green
Helen Chrysler Greene
The Alan C. Greenberg Foundation
Kathryn Greer
Guenther E. and Renate Greiner
Terri Grodner
Jan L. Gross in memory of Diane Gross
Audrey and Martin Gruss Foundation in honor of Karen LeFrak
Evelyn M. Guth
Paul Hallingby, Jr.
Virginia Sullivan Hampton
Joyce Harris
Mrs. Veronica Harris
Kelly A. Hatcher
Craig M. Hatkoff and Jane L. Rosenthal
Guy and Peggy Hauck
Darrell and Doreen Hayes
Gerry and Perren Hayes
Bruce J. Heim Foundation
Dave and Peggy Helming
Theresa S. Hensgen
Skip and Jervia Herendeen in memory of Maxwell Riddle
Ninette Herron
Jean Hetherington
Ronnie Heyman in honor of Karen LeFrak
Engine Co. #7, Hicksville Fire Department, in memory of Tom McCarthy
Gus N. Hinojosa, R.A.
Paul Hoffman
William and Janet Holbrook
Mara C. Holiday
Carol J. Hollands
The Janet A. Hooker Charitable Trust
Anthony A. Houston
Tonya and Teddy Howe
Howard G. Hubbard
Debra A. Iles
Jill Iscol
Kandie K. Isom
Desiree Jaeger
Jennifer Johnson
Lyle and Marjorie Johnson
The Robert W. Johnson IV Charitable Trust
Sale F. Johnson
Jasmina Kalamperovic
Peter Kalikow in honor of Karen LeFrak
Jason Karp
Anne Katona
George S. Kaufman in honor of Karen LeFrak
Kathy Kaye
Elisa Kelly
Dennis Kelty
Thomas A. Kilcullen
Barbara B. King
Paul and Linda Kline
Denise Kodner

Barbara Jane Kolk
Nan Kramer
Patricia Krause
The H. Frederick Krimendahl II Foundation
Mary-Lee Kvietkus
Bartley R. Labiner, DDS
S.C. LaBrecque
Jean Labriola
Linda M. Lacchia
Joan and Joe Lacey in honor of Karen LeFrak
R.F. Lagomarsino
Nancy J. Lang
Ed Lamberski
Gina DiNardo Lash and Marc D. Lash
Cristyne F. Lategano
Pat Laurans in memory of Pauline Tucker
Mr. and Mrs. Leonard D. Lauder
The Lauder Foundation
Patricia W. Laurans
Lisa Lawrence
Mr. and Mrs. William E. Leavitt in memory of Alex
Richard T. Leeolou
Janet E. Levy
Marian E. Levy
Samm Lewis
Chi-Ky Li
Lincoln Hills Duplicate Bridge Club
Michael A. Liosis
John Langloth Loeb, Jr.
Cynthia and Dan Lufkin
Kim Dung Luong
John Magliocco in honor of Karen LeFrak
Ninah and Michael Lynne in honor of Karen LeFrak
Gerard and Laura Mafale
Elizabeth Mahncke
Pamela Cooper-Manaton and Cary Manaton
Anne and Thomas Maness
Greg Martin
Nancy Matlock
Suzanne McKenna
Ian and Sonnet McKinnon
Juanita and Mary Beth McMullen in honor of Tresor Theresa Holt-McNulty
Ellen F. Meckler
Kelly J. Meehan
Patricia Meehan
Robert and Meryl Meltzer
Mrs. Barbara Miller
Connie G. Miller in memory of Fred T. Miller
Elizabeth and Victor Miller
Phyllis Jackson Mills
Howard P. Milstein Foundation
Barbara Moore
Barbara Anne Moore
Linda C. More
Chappy Morris
W.H. Morrison
Albert and Cynthia Musciano
Carol J. Murray
Ellen Jo Myers
Carmen R. Nassar
Greg and Donna Newsome
Daniel Nitschke
Brenda Nix and Donna Pintye in memory of Odie
Adrienne O'Brien
Barbara Ohmann
Daisy L. Okas
Marie E. O'Neill
Margaret O'Reilly in memory of Shannon, Stephanie and Jeffrey Ortel
Rosanne Ott
Pamela and Edward Pantzer
Pamela Pantzer
Sandra Parente in honor of John A. Parente
Rajshree S. Patel
Kenneth J. Patrick
Susan Patricof
Toni Peebler
Willie Perry
Alira Phillips
PH&L Co #1 Hicksville Fire Department
Jewell Pickens on behalf of Nicole and John Pickens
Robin Pickett in honor of Karen LeFrak
Stephanie Pier
Eileen Pimlott
Michael Pinero
Amanda M. Pough in honor of Margaret B. Pough
Pauline and Morgan Radler
Gabriel and Ivonne Rangel
Samuel and Estelle Rauch
Ron and Suzanne Readmond
Bill Rechler
David Reed
Vicki and Peter Rees
Linda Reinle
Honi Reisman
Karen Reuter
Darlene M. Rich
Wendy Richardson
Elaine Ridgen
Melvin Rivera
David and Ellen Roberts
Gary S. Robinson
Maria Robinson
Chris Rogers
Marshall Rose
Mr. and Mrs. Jonathan P. Rosen
Kathryn N. Rowcroft
Susan Rudin
Candace Russell
Emilia A. Saint-Amand
Samual Saleem
Dolores A. Salvi
Stephen and Leslie Sax
Kathleen Scherle
Lowell M. Schulman
Bernard and Francine Schwartz
Mr. and Mrs. Stephen A. Schwarzman
Herbert and Hermine Scolnik
Virginia and Raymond Scott
Patricia Scully
Ann Sergi
Mrs. Marlene Shaefer
Irving Shafran in honor of Karen LeFrak
Thomas and Ashley Sharp
Susan B. Sherman
Johnny Shoemaker in memory of Tom Conway
Silvia Sigman
Nancy and Henry Silverman
Neil R. Singer
Robert H. Slay
Don and Elaine Sloan
Lovelyne Smith
Polly and Robert Smith
Larry Sorenson
Paul and Daisy Soros Foundation
William and Matilda Speck
Peggy Speed
Maria Spencer
Denis Springer
Dennis and Susan Sprung
Matthew H. Stander
Robin Stansell
Robert and Helen Stein
Allison Stern in honor of Karen LeFrak
Ethan Stern and Family
Charlotte St. Martin
Jackson Steele
James T. and Andrea Stevens
Daphna Straus and Michael Bernstein
The Bachman Strauss Family Fund in memory of Pauline Tucker
Bonnie and Tom Strauss in honor of Karen LeFrak
Christine Strom
David and Dinae Squirrell
Michael J. Suave
Alice Suriani
Michael F. Swick
Angelita Tay
Tina Thomas
The Laurie Tisch Sussman Foundation
Barbara and Donald Tober
Jacqueline Tomkovich
D. Kay and Ralph G. Tripp
Donald Trump
Pauline Tucker in honor of Karen LeFrak
Cieolo Vacula
Mr. and Mrs. Frederick Vanacore
M. VandenBergh
Michelle Veasey
Cynthia and David Vogels
Dawndolyn Walden
Ellen M. Walsh
Isabel Walsh
Jack Waltz
Larry and Donna Warsoff
Helma N. Weeks
Hilde Weihermann
James Weingartner
Andrew H. and Susan B. Weinstein
Jerrold and Adele Weissman in memory of Shike Goldblatt
Ina West
Lorraine West
John and Charlotte White
Wendy and Paul Willhauck
Wendy D. Williams
Kim Winston
Ruth Winston
Susan Elaine Winter
Betty Winthers in loving memory of Michele Simpson
Jean S. and Hugh M. Witt III
Meredith Wollins
John W. Woods
Reva Wurtzburger
Thasneem Yao
The Janet Stone Jones Foundation on behalf of Janet York
Robert and Cindy Young
Eugene Z. Zaphiris

DOGNY has received Sponsorships and Contributions from companies and individuals that wish to remain anonymous.

Index of Artists

Index of Sculptures

DOGNY — America's Tribute to Search and Rescue Dogs. A gift from The American Kennel Club to The City of New York in recognition of the dogs who served America on September 11, 2001.

The AKC Board of Directors

Ronald H. Menaker, Chairman
Hon. David C. Merriam, Vice Chairman

Dr. Carmen L. Battaglia
Dr. Thomas M. Davies
Dr. J. Charles Garvin
Steven D. Gladstone
Walter F. Goodman
Robert L. Kelly
Kenneth A. Marden
Dr. Asa Mays
Patricia Scully
Nina Schaefer
Patti L. Strand

Alfred L. Cheauré, President, ex officio

DOGNY Honorary Chairmen

Honorable George E. Pataki, *Governor of New York State*
Honorable Michael R. Bloomberg, *Mayor of New York City*
Honorable Rudolph W. Giuliani, *Former Mayor of New York City*
Honorable Raymond W. Kelly, *Commissioner of the NYPD*
Honorable Nicholas Scoppetta, *Commissioner of the FDNY*

DOGNY Co-Chairs

Karen LeFrak, *Lefrak Organization*
Ronald H. Menaker, *Chairman, AKC*
Dennis B. Sprung, *Vice President, AKC*

DOGNY Committee

Jeff Ansell, *President, IAMS*
Dr. Carmen L. Battaglia, *President, AKC CAR*
Alfred L. Cheauré, *President & CEO, AKC*
John Daniello, *JGD Associates*
Robert Devine, *President, Hartz Corporation*
Eric Friedberg
Thomas A. Grabe, *Publisher, Canine Chronicle*
Gilbert S. Kahn
Marsha Levine, *Marlborough Gallery*
Iris Love
Ken A. May, *Sr. Vice President, FedEx*
Randy Mastro, *Partner, Gibson, Dunn & Crutcher*
Cristyne L. Nicholas, *President, NYC & Company*
Scott Rechler, *Co-CEO, Reckson Associates*
Howard Rubenstein, *President, Rubenstein Associates*
Liz Smith, *Columnist*
Toni Sosnoff, *Atalanta Sosnoff*
Matthew H. Stander, *Dog News*
Jonathan M. Tisch, *Chairman, NYC & Company*
Carl Weisbrod, *President, Alliance for Downtown New York, Inc.*